Revising

Jane Harper Yarbrough

Revising

New Essays for Teachers of Writing

Ronald A. Sudol, Editor
Oakland University

ERIC Clearinghouse on Reading and Communication Skills
National Institute of Education

National Council of Teachers of English
1111 Kenyon Road, Urbana, Illinois, 61801

NCTE Editorial Board: Paul T. Bryant, Marilyn Hanf Buckley, Thomas L. Clark, Jane M. Hornburger, Zora Rashkis, Robert F. Hogan, *ex officio,* Paul O'Dea, *ex officio*

Book Design: Tom Kovacs

NCTE Stock Number 41269

Published 1982 by the ERIC Clearinghouse on Reading and Communication Skills and the National Council of Teachers of English, 1111 Kenyon Road, Urbana, Illinois 61801

This publication was prepared with funding from the National Institute of Education, U.S. Department of Education, under contract no. 400-78-0026. Contractors undertaking such projects under government sponsorship are encouraged to express freely their judgment in professional and technical matters. Prior to publication, the manuscript was submitted to the Editorial Board of the National Council of Teachers of English for critical review and determination of professional competence. This publication has met such standards. Points of view or opinions, however, do not necessarily represent the official view or opinions of either the National Council of Teachers of English or the National Institute of Education.

Library of Congress Cataloging in Publication Data

Main entry under title:
Revising: new essays for teachers of writing.
    Bibliography: p.
    1. English language—Rhetoric—Study and teaching—Addresses, essays, lectures.   2. English language—Style—Addresses, essays, lectures.
3. Editing—Addresses, essays, lectures.   I. Sudol, Ronald A., 1943-   .   II. National Council of Teachers of English.
PE1404.R45   1982   808'.042'071173   82-8021
ISBN 0-8141-4126-9   (National Council of Teachers of English)   AACR2

Contents

Foreword

The Educational Resources Information Center (ERIC) is a national information system developed by the U.S. Office of Education and now sponsored by the National Institute of Education (NIE). It provides ready access to descriptions of exemplary programs, to research and development efforts, and to related information useful in developing more effective educational programs.

Through its network of specialized centers or clearinghouses, each of which is responsible for a particular educational area, ERIC acquires, evaluates, abstracts, and indexes current information and lists that information in its reference publications.

The ERIC Clearinghouse on Reading and Communication Skills (ERIC/RCS) disseminates educational information related to research, instruction, and personnel preparation at all levels and in all institutions. The scope of interest of the Clearinghouse includes relevant research reports, literature reviews, curriculum guides and descriptions, conference papers, project or program reviews, and other print materials related to all aspects of reading, English, educational journalism, and speech communication.

The ERIC system has already made available—through the ERIC Document Reproduction System—much informative data. However, if the findings of specific educational research are to be used by teachers, much of the data must be translated into an essentially different context. Rather than resting at the point of making research reports easily accessible, NIE has directed the separate ERIC clearinghouses to work with professional organizations in developing information analysis papers in specific areas within the scope of the clearinghouses.

ERIC is pleased to cooperate with the National Council of Teachers of English in making *Revising: New Essays for Teachers of Writing* available.

Bernard O'Donnell
Director, ERIC/RCS

Introduction

Most teachers of writing, I suspect, have found that ten minutes spent guiding a student's revision of one paper can be more valuable than several hours of classroom activities and grading. No theory, no hypothetical examples, no models by professional writers, no cryptic marginal comments—just critical attention focused on the student's own work in a mutual effort to make it better. And having made it "better," and then experiencing an all-too-rare sense of accomplishment, we try to discover how to achieve such results more efficiently. It is no wonder, then, that in our principal journals and at our professional meetings the number of articles and papers concerning revising has increased noticeably. This book adds sixteen new essays to the growing list, and I know the authors join me in hoping that this collection brings us closer to understanding how to help students effectively revise their work.

When we think about revising as something students may—or may not—do to the drafts of their papers, we probably imagine a specific activity or a particular stage in the writing process. But research into the behavior of writers and our own observations suggest that revising encompasses many activities and is not limited to the last stages in the writing process. Thus we encounter a problem of definition: our casual use of the term is somewhat different from our professional use of it. That is, when we examine revising as teachers and researchers, we find it to be related to almost everything else we know about writing. None of the essays here attempts a formal definition of revising, but the essays as a group point to the problem of definition. As a subject of study by teachers and researchers, revising acquires definition according to its identification with such related concerns as editing, thinking, teaching, and learning.

Editing requires the use of rules, maxims, and common sense to produce an error-free text suitable for reading. The most easily detected problems with student writing are lapses of effective revision of this kind—deviation from expected standards of usage and mechanics, poor lexical and syntactic choices, a general inattentiveness to the small repairs that can smooth the surface of

ix

a final draft. Although most teachers today probably give basic editing much less emphasis than other features of writing, the fact remains that many of the controversies that involve members of the National Council of Teachers of English hinge on the nature of students' final drafts. The nonsexist use of language, the students' rights to their own language, the back-to-basics movement, the use of placement testing, the evaluation of writing, the definition of remedial writing, the literacy crisis—these issues and others are concerned quite directly with how students edit their work.

While these controversies have raged over the written products of our students, scholars of rhetoric and composition have been examining the whole writing process, providing a second context for a definition of revising—that is, revising as the exercise of critical thinking to induce fresh discovery. The principle that has emerged from research into the composing process is that disciplined thinking and writing about the subject, situation, purpose, and audience of a piece of writing will improve the quality of the final product. Revising plays a role in this process by providing for critical intervention along the way. This is a dynamic and recursive action that allows the production of language itself to guide discovery.

A teacher's role in motivating students toward effective editing and creative thinking provides a third approach to the subject of revising. Guiding revision of a project already in progress may be a more manageable pedagogical task than guiding a student through the mysteries of invention. Insofar as revising consists of the practical application of accepted principles of rhetorical and stylistic effectiveness, a teacher transmits to a student the authority of the culture's tastes and values. And the teacher exercises this authority chiefly by becoming a surrogate audience in order to direct the student's revision. This is why teachers read and comment on student papers. When teachers read and comment on a series of first drafts that are never subsequently revised, the focus of their authority becomes judgment divorced from communicative function. The manner in which teachers communicate their authority is crucial to the success of their larger task and is a subject that presents opportunities for useful future research.

The fourth context for a definition of revising is that of learning itself, for learning rarely occurs except as the expansion or modification of what is already known. To satisfy intellectual curiosity, to master a skill or a body of knowledge, to strengthen belief, to change an opinion—these are revisionary acts that either answer critical doubt or reinforce acritical conviction. Revision is the essence of intellectual growth. It liberates us from confinement by narrow forms of thought and feeling, from mental laxity, and from whatever is old, false, tired, and trite. We all know how difficult it is to discard an idea or production that seems complete. In writing, the first draft tyrannizes the second unless revising becomes creative learning. The effects of this tyranny are well illustrated in an experiment reported on at the 1981 meeting of the Conference on College Composition and Communication. After a large number of students submitted essays on an assigned topic, they were asked to do the same assignment again. One group had access to their first versions; the other group did not. As might be expected, those in the second group altered the content of their work considerably and wrote better papers, while those who had access to their earlier drafts seemed, in general, to limit themselves to copyediting.

The essays collected here reflect all of these overlapping concerns and are arranged in two broad categories. The first six concern theoretical and intellectual backgrounds, including communication theory, cognitive psychology, the history of rhetoric, style analysis, and protocol analysis. The next ten discuss applications—curriculum, classroom strategies, techniques for revising words and sentences, the use of peer evaluation, and the dynamics of communication between teacher and student. The particular features of this design may be seen in the conceptual table of contents below and in the summary of the individual essays that follows.

According to Daniel Marder in "Revision as Discovery and the Reduction of Entropy" revising is an act of discovery accomplished through three overlapping considerations—text, writer, reader. He explores the metaphor of entropy in creating a "readerly text" by means of the ratio of meaningful complexity to meaningful redundancy. The essay—itself resonant with meaningful complexity—views revising as an act of creative imagination. A different compartment of the mind—cognitive function—is examined by Ellen W. Nold in "Revising: Intentions and Conventions." After identifying and classifying the subtasks of writing, she argues that the teaching of revising strategies should correspond to the student's level of achievement in cognitive subtasks, and that teachers may effectively relate drafts-in-progress to these stages of cognitive development.

In her survey "A History of Revision: Theory versus Practice" Karen Hodges shows how the narrow view of revision as "correction" has persisted in rhetorical theory through the ages despite the actual re-invention practices of writers. To compensate for the absence of a coherent theory of revision, she suggests we adapt Aristotle's topics of invention to "topics of revision," working toward a heuristic for transforming fragments into polished wholes. The methodology of professional writers described by Hodges is examined in particular detail by R. Baird Shuman in "H. G. Wells' *The Outline of History*: A Study of Revision." Shuman demonstrates how an author's or an editor's apparent stylistic tinkering affects the logic, clarity, and emphasis of content, how even the smallest revisions are acts of judgment, and how superior style succumbs to the need for prudent and exact expression.

Whereas Wells was a light reviser, the blind writer described by Anne Ruggles Gere in "Insights from the Blind" is a non-reviser. Gere shows how this writer, whose prodigious memory compensates for the loss of sight, is able to produce polished essays in the first draft. The blind writer's "insight" and ability to avoid the need to revise has implications for teaching—such as the revival of certain unfashionable pedagogies—and for research —such as that on the relationship of the senses to thought. In contrast, the mind of the extensive reviser is explored by Richard Beach in "The Pragmatics of Self-assessing." The extensive reviser infers audience knowledge, beliefs, attitudes, and so forth, and revises to subordinate excesses of self-expression to the exigencies of situation and purpose. In place of style-oriented maxims, Beach recommends "Grice's Maxims" on the exchange of information since they focus less attention on expression, more on effect. These pragmatic concerns foreshadow the second group of essays, those on applications.

In "A Holistic Pedagogy for Freshman Composition" Ruth Windhover identifies defects in the "studio" and "factory" classroom models and recommends adoption of a "workshop" model based on research in problem solving and primary traits evaluation. In this scheme revising is a recursive confrontation with the constraints on writing rather than part of a sequential process. One of these constraints is lack of motivation. In "Teaching Teachers to Teach Revision" Toby Fulwiler argues that a program of "writing across the curriculum" provides some of the practical imperatives by which students may be motivated to take the trouble to revise their work. Workshops for non-English faculty stress the connection between revising and rethinking as essential ingredients for success in various disciplines and careers.

The next three essays focus on revising at the word and sentence levels. In her essay "Psycholinguistic Perspectives on Revising" C. A. Daiute explains how short-term memory of grammatical details among basic writing students causes them to produce apparently misconnected sentences. In contrast to the reader-directed revising at the rhetorical level, help for these students should take the form of distinct segments in the composing process. One useful heuristic for sentence revision, according to Daiute, is "sector analysis." Ken Davis describes a classroom activity that encourages the evaluation and revision of words for readability in "The Cloze Test as a Diagnostic Tool for Revision." By removing words from student essays and then conducting a guessing game about what the missing words might be, Davis is able to demonstrate to students the need to account for readers' automatic predictions of upcoming words. A different problem with words is explored by Robert Gregory in his essay "On Parapraxes and Revision." Slips of the pen in an early draft, he contends, may suggest the writer's alienation from the topic or lack of genuine commitment to it. Correct interpretation of the slip may lead to successful revision.

The next two essays describe classroom activities that use peer evaluation as a basis for understanding revising. In "Revision and Improvement: Making the Connection" Gayle L. Smith shows what students can learn by trying to figure out the order of composition of three drafts of the same paper. Among the useful discoveries her students make is that writing sometimes gets worse before it gets better. Robert J. Denn describes a successful form of peer evaluation in "The Delphi Technique: Revising as Problem Solving." This technique eliminates the "noise" of open discussion because students respond to the drafts of other students anonymously and in writing.

The final three essays have to do with the dynamics of communication between teacher and student. In "Revision and Risk" John J. Ruszkiewicz observes that since the exercise of rhetorical choices does not guarantee improvement, students view revising as risky and therefore avoid it. The teacher should counteract this tendency, he says, by actually teaching revising and by insisting that students exercise choice and accept the consequent risks. In " 'But It's Just My Opinion': Understanding Conflict with Students about the Expression of Opinion" Edmund Miller examines the problem of students' failure to distinguish between revising for style and revising for content. He recommends methods by which students may be helped to see that a teacher's comments are usually directed toward improving the expression of ideas, not toward changing the ideas themselves. In "Empathy and Revision" Karen I. Spear argues that although teachers usually have an empathic attitude toward students with writing problems, they often fail to communicate it. In addition to serving as surrogate audience, the teacher should act as a therapist, helping the student clear the air for constructive criticism and assume primary responsibility for revision.

Charles R. Duke has performed a most valuable professional service by compiling the annotated bibliography, an indispensable tool for those interested in further study on revising. The bibliography provides a brief survey of commentary over the past decade.

Ronald A. Sudol

Background: Theory, History, and Cases

Revision as Discovery and the Reduction of Entropy

Daniel Marder
University of Tulsa

We tend to think of revision as a step in the writing process, perhaps even the final one; yet, a draft existed first in the mind and was redone, perhaps many times, before it was committed to paper. Even then it was altered in the very act of writing through deletions, substitutions, and additions. A first draft is already many drafts and what has come to be termed prewriting might well be considered rewriting, just as thinking cannot be distinguished from rethinking. Like Yeats, we find we cannot separate the dancer from the dance.

Revision as Discovery

What is the meaning of all these revisions? What is the writer doing? To Herman Melville the act of writing was a voyage into "the world of the mind" in search of a "golden haven," and if that haven was not gained, "better to sink in boundless deeps, than float on vulgar shoals. . . . Give me, ye gods," Melville concluded, "an utter wreck, if wreck I do."[1] Not all writers consider the job so dangerous, but it would be difficult to find one who has not understood the act of writing as one of discovery. In a recent article, Donald M. Murray quotes dozens of writers who agree that the process of revision is one of discovery, among them Mary McCarthy, who observes, "Every short story, at least for me, is a little act of discovery. A cluster of details presents itself to my scrutiny, like a mystery that I will understand in the course of writing or sometimes not fully until afterward."[2] Poe concurs, noting that in "The Raven" he discovered along the way the effects he wished to produce.[3] When his mental image of those effects changed, he undertook another revision. Ultimately, as he revised, he achieved a written version of that image.

But such resolution is not always the case. Many writers never feel that a work is completed, and they rearrange, delete, add, and

3

substitute through the final page proofs. As the *Paris Review* interviews so clearly document, writers view rewriting as a process of discovery. Indeed, if writers already knew what they were going to say and merely said it, they would be bored. Writing would be a chore instead of a challenge. As Mary McCarthy puts it, "A story that you do not learn something from while you are writing it, that does not illuminate something for you, is dead, finished before you started it."[4]

Knowing what one is going to say and then saying it, however, may well be the practice of most utilitarian writers—and the source of their writing difficulties. These writers tend to report and explain what they already know in technical and scientific reports, business papers, letters, legal briefs, and the front-page news. The piece has been worked out—the relationships made, the graphs drawn, the conclusions reached—before the writer begins to report or explain or argue. Writers of stories or poems, on the other hand, seldom talk about their work before it happens because they fear that discovery may occur when they are not ready for it, as they are talking rather than while they are writing. They will be unable to go back to the prediscovery stage to reshape the material again and again until they discover its final form—the order which *is* its meaning. It may even happen in the various stages of rewriting that writers discover meaning in a direction they did not intend to pursue. "Thought goes as it will," Jules Renard observed. "As it follows the pen, it loses its freedom. It wants to go one way, the pen another. It is like a blind man led astray by his cane, and what I came to write is no longer what I wished to write."[5]

Strictures in composition texts can hardly be applied to the events that occur while pressing our thoughts on paper because they would interfere with the hot flow of thought. The precise word, the correct tense, the exact formulation, the deliberate choice of analogy or simile or descriptive phrase, the arrangement of a sentence for more dramatic effect or closer relationship with the previous one—all these efforts are revisionary. They are still means of discovery, however, and often result in the entire recasting of the composition to accommodate what has been discovered.

As a writer discovers through revision the style and form, the order which is ultimately meaning, he or she begins to hypothesize a model of the argument or description or explanation, and that model tends to guide the further expansion of the composition. Upon reading the draft or a part of it, however, the writer may find that the model was not followed or that it was not really what was wanted after all; and the writer may begin again, or take an aberrant piece of writing from the draft and build upon that, using a second hypothesis derived from the first, a third derived from the second, and so on until something approaching the writer's satisfaction is achieved. In this process there is often no distinction between utilitarian and artistic writing. The scientist with an array of disparate data may set out to discuss each table and graph without perceiving the relationships that give order and meaning, just as the creative writer may offer myriad experiences and associations without apparent order, both writers finding justification, perhaps unconsciously, in the prevailing attitude that sees as absurd the classical methods of exposition—of relating, defining, classifying, and analyzing. Such forms for discovering what to say and expanding upon it seem to imply a rigidity that limits or denies discovery when "logic is not the way things work at all." Whether the universe is logical or not, human endeavor is based on the assumption of meaning; and writers must achieve a coherent and convincing view of the way things are—even if they discover that way to be ultimately meaningless.

Everything external to the writer has order and meaning imposed upon it—or discovered within it—by the writer. (The difference is a philosophical point that for this discussion must remain a digression.) To the extent that readers perceive that order and thus comprehend its meaning, whether they take it as fiction or truth, the writer has communicated. The assumption in all utilitarian writing is that order must be perceived, not invented, and it is to the revision of utilitarian prose we now turn.

The Writer as Reader

As I have argued elsewhere, the writer's motive is more or less persuasive.[6] If readers already share much of what the writer is saying, or if their emotional, intellectual, and cultural patterns are similar, then obviously less persuasion is necessary. More is necessary as the information becomes more remote from the reader's experience. This observation appears obvious, and perhaps that is why it is so often ignored; yet, it is the ultimate reduction of all writing situations. To the extent culture is shared, reality can be agreed upon, and the writer may refer to an established agreement. At the other end of the spectrum, the writer may have to argue with inventive powers in order to bring an audience into agreement with the writer's view. Evidence, logic, and the experience of living are the writer's major means. A mere description of a bridge does not require much persuasion, since a reader can check it by observation and will generally trust the writer, unless the writer destroys his or her credibility with displays of bad manners (again an agreement) through such obvious errors as grammatical and spelling mistakes. But the reader may need considerably more persuasion to agree about the best place to put the bridge or the design it ought to have or whether or not it ought to be built. Along the entire spectrum, then, all is persuasion, even at the factual end, where one interpretation is shared at the outset.

In poetry and fiction and perhaps very personal essays, the reader is taken through the experiences of the writer and thus discovers meaning as the writer discovered it, by accumulation. In utilitarian prose, however, the meaning is stated, whether inductively or deductively or both, and the burden of composition is substantiating or reinforcing or rendering that meaning. After a draft has been completed—that is, after the writer has gone through the various revisions to get to an initial ending—he or she becomes a reader and may find that the efforts at persuasion (at substantiating or reinforcing or rendering) do not provide the desired effect, that the perceived order of things cannot be made convincing. In that event, the order must be changed to correspond with the generalizations and meanings that can be substantiated. The image of order we have held in mind must now change to suit ourselves as reader of ourselves.[7]

As we test the persuasive power of what we have written, we rewrite, relying on the standard though ancient methods of description, narration, classification, analysis, and so on, and on our mental models of effective style. In the rewriting process, however, these techniques of organization and style become more conscious; we apply what we know of them, making them more complete and more logical. It is this conscious attention that we deliberately sacrificed in the first rush of invention. The experienced writer usually employs these techniques by habit, without specific awareness, but he or she nevertheless reapplies them in revision; the less experienced writer will not have acquired these techniques as habit and will therefore find much more to rewrite and consequently to discover in the process of revision.

In the revision process a writer discovers more than meanings and the inseparable ways of rendering them. There is also the matter of stylistic propensities. Does the writer tend to abstractions or concreteness? Does the writer avoid details or detail the obvious? Is the tendency to successive long sentences or short ones? Are the paragraphs series of periodic sentences or loose ones? Or, as in so many technological reports, are complex sentences piled upon complex sentences, wearying the reader's ability to concentrate? Does the writer tend to digress or is there a stingy chariness? Is there a tendency to aggregate or segregate thought so that a paragraph extends over five manuscript pages or five paragraphs are set upon a single page? Is there a strong inclination to the passive or an overexcited reliance on the active? An adherence to static description or the unrelieved activity of narration? Does the writer plunge on without summary or is there a maddening summation at the end of every few sentences, with the effect of two steps forward and one back? Is the writer's propensity monotonously deductive or inductive? These questions asked during revision are of course the same questions asked during writing, but once writers have discerned their stylistic propensities, they can either reinforce them or change them to achieve the effect they wish. Of course, writers must have read enough, be educated enough, to have a mental model of writing that will be effective to others and against which they can test the persuasive powers of what they have written.

Reader-oriented Revision and the Metaphor of Entropy

While writers are seeking order or meaning, they cannot devote full attention to the reader. Nor can they totally listen to themselves as readers if they are busy discovering propensities to style and form and consequently changing or developing thought and composition habits. Attention to the reader must be a conscious act in itself, apart from all previous writing activity. Again, the utilitarian writer thinks differently than the poet or fiction writer who is often trying to express the inexpressible and seldom aiming for a direct denotative strike at a singular meaning in the minds of a specific audience. Such writing is, according to most accounts, aimed at the writer's own image of his or her cognitions. Unfortunately, the utilitarian writer, especially in the academies and the professions, often acts in much the same way as the esthetic writer, forgetting the audience in a display of acuteness and profundity. As a result, these writers, although printing hundreds, even thousands, of copies of their work, may communicate with only a handful of their colleagues.

This situation has become all too familiar in the twentieth century with its proliferation of technology and bureaucracy. But we would do well to remember that it was not unfamiliar in the seventeenth century when the Royal Society condemned puffed language, nor in the eighteenth when George Campbell in *The Philosophy of Rhetoric* distinguished between a "languid" style and a "vivacious" one. The one is subject- or writer-oriented, achieving the writer's meaning without much regard for the reader; the other is reader-oriented. In *The Philosophy of Composition,* E. D. Hirsch speaks of "relative readability," a term that suggests a range between writer-oriented and reader-oriented possibilities.[8] The "relative readability" of Campbell's "vivacious" style would be high, over toward the reader-oriented end of the range. And it is this end of the range that should attract the attention of the writer of a utilitarian text in the last stage of revision.[9]

A useful device in discussing the last stage of revision is the metaphor of entropy, a metaphor that promises a systematic means of achieving Campbell's "vivacious" style in the process of revision by reducing the reader's sense of disorder in the text and allowing the writer's meaning to be perceived, to live in the reader's sensibility. A complex text dense with unfamiliar information is more likely to threaten than to communicate with a reader. Such a text can be considered a high entropy system, and the writer's object is to reduce the entropy. To do so, the writer must invade the system with new ordering energy, or negative entropy.

Originally, entropy was a thermodynamic metaphor, but it has been adapted to communications theory and is well established. In thermodynamics, the effort to reduce the entropy of a system— to make it more orderly—is considered an unnatural process, and it must be accompanied by a natural process, which is the increasing of energy elsewhere, outside the system. The processes of nature compensate for the processes of human beings, which means that the tendency of the universe is always toward the human conception of disorder, which we naturally abhor. This aspect of entropy, however, is ignored when the metaphor is applied to communications theory. Here, entropy is the measure of randomness in the information, which is a neat application of the thermodynamic definition of entropy as a measure of the random motion of molecules. Meaning in communications theory is the ordering of information transmitted through a medium or channel. All bits of information in the channel that are not received or read as meaning become noise. If the receiver of the information has a high degree of freedom in selecting meaning, then the entropy is high, which means the information is largely noise; it is loosely organized or even shapeless. (Literary works that aim at suggestion and ambiguity would be intentionally high entropy systems.) Entropy increases not only with noise but with density of information, particles of possible meaning crowded in a channel at too high a rate for the receiver's decoding ability.

Entropy is combated, on the other hand, by redundancies, which allow the receiver to anticipate and thus make meaningful what will be said next. The more redundancy found in a system, the greater its tolerance for noise. This theory obviously involves a good deal of counting and it may be of value in communications that aim at absolute denotation, as in mathematical language. But even in reports, a genre of discourse forever fighting the connotative nature of language, we find the shaping of reason, a process involving generalizations, abstractions, complex turns of thought. Even if these qualities could be counted, their values would change in each use; all subordinations, for instance, would not be equal.

Communications theory has developed its metaphor most obviously from analogy with electronic systems where the random motion of electrons in conductors, transistors, and the like are indicators of disorder. Here the tendency to high entropy is always bad news and its reduction good. When we apply the metaphor to rhetoric, however, we find that high entropy may serve useful purposes, especially in literary works that aim at the representation of an ambiguous universe or intend a great deal of suggestiveness and wide connotation, or in phenomenological exercises. In the process of revising utilitarian texts, however, the writer should always seek to reduce the entropy.

The writer is the ordering force, the negative entropy invading the system which now consists of the text and the reader. (Whether or not the process increases the writer's own entropy as a result of the writer's input to the text-reader system is not significant in our use of the metaphor.) A text may be by nature highly complex, difficult for pertinent readers and impossible for others; that is, the text and its audience may be by nature a highly entropic system. Many professional and sophisticated audiences might be bored if the text were not complicated enough to attract their lively attention, to offer them something new. Nevertheless, the writer in revising attempts to lower the entropy to the extent possible by simplifying the complex. Quite often, however, a writer tends for various personal reasons to raise the entropy by complicating the simple.

Use of the entropy metaphor in the revising process has precedent in the popular eighteenth-century rhetoric of Hugh Blair. He speaks of the relationship in a piece of rhetoric between the familiar and the strange. The proportion or perhaps we may say the ratio of the familiar to the strange determines the degree of order in the system—of course, Blair does not talk about systems as do theorists in communication. Blair's idea of the strange, which includes highly abstract words or far-reaching metaphors —whatever is unfamiliar—accounts for types and degrees of audience ability to read or understand. Although Blair's idea of the strange is more inclusive than the idea of new information in communications theory, it is still insufficient for an understanding of entropy in rhetoric. There is at least one more factor that works against the reader's ability to recreate the writer's meaning.

The additional factor is the density of relationships such as ambiguities, coordinations, subordinations, modifications, and degrees of digression, including associative processes, non sequiturs, and other alogical juxtapositions. For rhetorical systems, therefore, we may say that entropy increases with the unfamiliarity of content, with the levels of abstraction, and with the density of relationships.

The ordering energy that the writer applies from outside the text-reader system in the process of revision must obviously render the unfamiliar familiar—and that rendering is fundamentally accomplished through redundancies. The writer may repeat parts of complex sentences in order to make two or three new sentences, each with less density; the writer may shape disparate ideas and observations by applying generalizations; the writer may appeal to the reader's knowledge by particularizing generalization with familiar details, analogies, or examples. Definition is a redundancy for the term defined; analysis is a redundancy for the structure under investigation; description is a redundancy for the term described. The idea of *rendering* is itself the idea of redundancy as opposed to statement. So is explanation with its various ways of saying one thing and of summarizing. The various devices of redundancy are the ways the writer delivers his or her meaning to the reader's understanding in all discourse, whether utilitarian or artistic. The rhythm, rhyme, assonance, and alliteration of poetry are devices of redundancy. Motif and symbol in fiction as well as poetry are easily recognized redundancies. Dominant moods also result from redundant elements in description. Myth itself is redundance that echoes through the centuries of a civilization.

Noise, defined as meaningless information in communications systems, is also a useful metaphor in the revision of rhetorical systems. Circumlocutions and clichés, excessive summary and the rendition of the obvious, lose the attention of a mature audience. They are all noise. But so are new items of information that remain unfamiliar and dense series of abstractions because they frustrate and ultimately tire the reader, who is always seeking meaning. Although noise does increase the tendency to disorder, we cannot make it fit neatly into a definition of entropy unless we distinguish between meaningful and meaningless redundancy. We can settle this troublesome detail by recognizing that excessive redundancy for a particular audience tends to become noise, just as unfathomable information is noise. In revision, as in all other aspects of the writing process, the writer must be guided by an image of the audience.

The writer who revises without particular attention to noise may not realize how it annoys the reader, just as misspellings, awkwardness, and violation of anticipated grammatical construction annoy the reader. Noise inadvertently establishes its own tone and thus subverts the reader's perception of the writer's attitude. What was intended as sincerity may come across as pompous vacuity, and the subtle insight may be received as unschooled ignorance.

As with excessive redundancies, new relationships can also become noise—meaningless combinations of information. Yet the very point of relationship is to create meaning, and content is shaped by relationships such as predication, coordination, subordination, and modification. A high density of any form of these relationships without variety or reinforcement, however, fails to accumulate into meaning. Similarly, abstractions and intended ambiguities are relationships in themselves and function as do all other relationships to establish meaning. Abstractions are generalizations that represent details; ambiguities are contradictory possibilities of meaning in a given situation. But like the others, these relationships also become noise when presented in excessive density.

To adapt the metaphor of entropy to the revision of rhetorical systems, we can employ the term "meaningful complexity" to represent all the factors that tend to abet disorder. We can then apply the term "meaningful redundancy" to the factors that the writer introduces to reduce disorder. It then becomes possible to represent in a single equation all the rhetorical factors that work to lower or raise entropy in the process of revision:

$$\text{Entropy} = \frac{\text{meaningful complexity and noise}}{\text{meaningful redundancy}}$$

Although we can phrase such an equation, the application of numerical values would be disastrous. Entropy, we must remember, is a metaphor. It is a metaphor in thermodynamics and in chemistry and a metaphor upon a metaphor in communications theory. Our adaption of the metaphor to rhetorical systems is in terms of tendency, which must be felt rather than calculated because rhetorical systems are composed of kinds of relationships that are not perceived by counting. Used qualitatively, the entropy equation can guide writers in ordering their critical sensibilities for the revision of written texts. It may also lead to a better description of the nature of rhetorical activity than we have had, and thus to more cogent means of analyzing a piece of rhetoric, whether established or in process.

Notes

1. Quoted from chapter 169, "Sailing On," in *Mardi*.

2. Donald M. Murray, "Internal Revision: A Process of Discovery," in *Research on Composing: Points of Departure,* eds. Charles R. Cooper and Lee Odell (Urbana, Ill.: National Council of Teachers of English, 1978), p. 102.

3. Edgar Allan Poe, "The Philosophy of Composition," in *Selected Writings of Edgar Allan Poe,* ed. Edward H. Davidson (Boston: Houghton Mifflin Co., Riverside Editions, 1956), pp. 452-63.

4. Cited in Murray, p. 102.

5. Ibid.

6. "The Spectrum of Rhetoric," *College Composition and Communication* 25 (May 1974): 181-85.

7. "Every human word implies not only the existence—at least in the imagination—of another to whom the word is uttered, but it also implies that the speaker has a kind of otherness within himself. He participates in this other to whom he speaks, and it is this underlying participation which makes communication possible...." Walter J. Ong, *The Barbarian Within and Other Fugitive Essays and Studies* (New York: Macmillan Co., 1962), p. 52.

8. For a comparison of Hirsch and Campbell, see Richard Dillman, "Hirsch and Campbell," *Rhetoric Society Quarterly* 9, no. 2 (Spring 1979): 92-96.

9. A utilitarian text—one that refers to the external universe—is a "readerly text" as some semioticists now call it, as opposed to a "writerly text." See, for example, Roland Barthes, *S-Z,* trans. Richard Miller (New York: Hill & Wang; Farrar, Straus & Giroux, 1974).

Revising:
Intentions and Conventions

Ellen W. Nold
Stanford University

In complex cognitive tasks like writing, people plan their behavior, perform the task, and review their performance. Metacognition is the label cognitive psychologists have given to this review of the product of mental effort (Flavell, 1977). Linguists have also arrived at a similar idea, and Bates (1974) speaks of "metapragmatics," the ability to analyze a message. Using the terminology of psychologists and linguists, then, we can say that the ability to revise rests on the writer's metacommunicative or metapragmatic abilities. As Flavell speculates,

> Metacommunication ability, like other "metas," is likely to be fairly late-developing. . . . One late-developing behavior is carefully shaping and tailoring a message under novel, unfamiliar conditions or constraints. . . . If you have to "solve" a "communication problem," rather than just "say what comes naturally". . . then you may have to consciously analyze, evaluate and edit candidate messages. Similarly, if your listener indicates that he did not understand your message, you may have to reanalyze and reevaluate it in order to construct a more adequate one. In both cases you are thinking about the message (metacommunication) rather than sending it (communication). (p. 178)

Revising writing is more difficult than reformulating speech because the audience is usually not available for help. Rather, writers must themselves act as intended audience. They do so because they blame the message, not the audience, when communication breaks down.

Recent research has shown that the ability to examine a message for faults and the ability to take the role of audience develop late. Markman (1977) found that young children are unlikely to recognize the inadequacy of instructions given them, a finding that supports Robinson's (1977) observation that young children

13

are likely to blame the listener, not the speaker, when instructions fail to communicate. Cooper and Flavell (1972; reported in Glucksberg, Krauss, and Higgins, 1975) note that many sixth-graders are aware that they should take the role of audience, though they cannot do so consistently, a finding supported by Crowhurst (1977), who found that sixth-graders do not significantly alter sentence structure to suit their audience—whether writing to a best friend or to a teacher; tenth-graders, however, made accommodations. Even so, as teachers well know, many college students do not unerringly meet the needs of their readers. In exploring the notion of Flavell and his colleagues (1968) that speakers first organize messages for themselves and then revise for an audience, Flower (1979) describes the structure and style of the "writer-based prose" of college students as opposed to their "reader-based prose." However promising this avenue of investigation may prove, the concept of role-taking ability has not yet been defined precisely enough to predict whether a given writer will be able to communicate well. The work of Scardamalia, Bereiter, and McDonald (1977) is a step in this direction.

Assumptions

In discussing the nature of writing and revision, I share four assumptions about cognitive functioning with Shatz (1978). The first is that cognitive resources are limited. George Miller (1956), for instance, notes that our short-term memory, the "space" available in focal attention, appears to be limited to between five and nine items. The second assumption, closely related to the first, is that this limited capacity can be stretched to do more work. Miller also points out that we "chunk" information together. For instance, the prepositional phrase "on the roof" is not remembered as three separate words but as one chunk—coded, perhaps non-linguistically, for retrieval (Kintsch, 1975). The third assumption is that each of the subtasks of a complex cognitive task demands a portion of the total resources (attention) available for cognitive processing. A subtask's load on attention (workload) is determined by two factors: how well we have learned it and how much attention we decide to give to it. Thus, we may reduce the workload of ill-learned subtasks by ignoring them, but if we do, the quality of our performance may be low. The fourth assumption is that in order to accomplish a complex cognitive task we pay attention to combinations of subtasks. The combined workload of the subtasks at any moment, however, cannot exceed our total space in focal attention. By judicious use of limited cognitive *space* over *time,* however, we can handle workloads that exceed our available space at any one moment. Thus, we can increase our ability to handle complex cognitive tasks by making some subtasks routine and by using strategies that ensure attention to all subtasks over the course of time. Attentional *space* does not usually grow over a lifetime; we merely attend *longer* (as our attention span increases) and *better* (as our knowledge and strategies increase).

Young children, however, are triply hampered in performing a complex task like writing: even twenty minutes on the task is too long, even the basic motor skills are not routine, and even the simplest metacognitive strategies are beyond them. Werner and Kaplan (1950) show that children do not spontaneously adopt consistent strategies to solve complex problems; rather, as White-hurst (1976) observes, they start *doing* a problem, unconcerned with planning or reviewing. One reason that children do not feel the need for strategy-making may be that they overestimate their cognitive abilities (Flavell, Friedrichs, and Hoyt, 1970). Naive about how limited their cognitive space is, children act as if it were equal to any task at any moment.

As Shatz (1978) points out, the four assumptions made here lead to insights about variation in the display of ability to handle a complex task, a variation that has plagued both cognitive psychologists and teachers:

> A skill is likely to appear sporadically depending on the degree of competence with it and other techniques called for in a given task. A particular skill will be revealed most readily when other cognitive demands are minimized. Conversely, the performance of a skill will be most degraded when the task which requires it makes other heavy processing demands. (pp. 9-10)

Writing: A Complex Task

Let us for the moment accept that writing is a complex task comprised of many subtasks. On what subtasks do writers spend their attention when they write? I have grouped ten subtasks into three categories: conventional, intentional, and mixed (Figure 1). Conventional subtasks can be learned early in the development of writing skills because they do not require decisions about audience, topic, or purpose. In fact, conventions may even be learned apart from the production of a message. Adults who are learning conventions learn motor skills faster than children because adults have learned other, similar skills; however, they have less advantage in learning graphical and usage subtasks. Conventions usually take very little of a skilled writer's attention (unless, for instance, the writer is just learning to type). Conventional subtasks are also less likely than mixed subtasks to suffer when writers are taxed by the demands of determining their intentions.

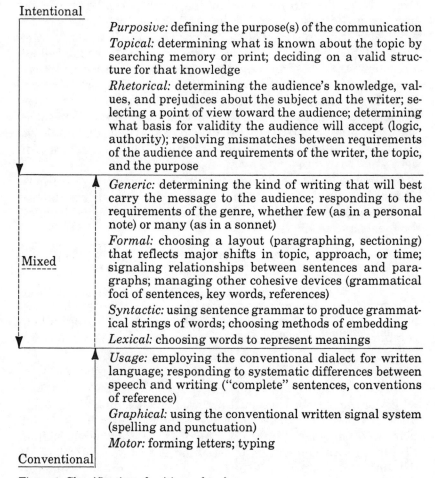

Intentional

Purposive: defining the purpose(s) of the communication

Topical: determining what is known about the topic by searching memory or print; deciding on a valid structure for that knowledge

Rhetorical: determining the audience's knowledge, values, and prejudices about the subject and the writer; selecting a point of view toward the audience; determining what basis for validity the audience will accept (logic, authority); resolving mismatches between requirements of the audience and requirements of the writer, the topic, and the purpose

Mixed

Generic: determining the kind of writing that will best carry the message to the audience; responding to the requirements of the genre, whether few (as in a personal note) or many (as in a sonnet)

Formal: choosing a layout (paragraphing, sectioning) that reflects major shifts in topic, approach, or time; signaling relationships between sentences and paragraphs; managing other cohesive devices (grammatical foci of sentences, key words, references)

Syntactic: using sentence grammar to produce grammatical strings of words; choosing methods of embedding

Lexical: choosing words to represent meanings

Usage: employing the conventional dialect for written language; responding to systematic differences between speech and writing ("complete" sentences, conventions of reference)

Graphical: using the conventional written signal system (spelling and punctuation)

Motor: forming letters; typing

Conventional

Figure 1. Classification of writing subtasks.

Writers develop skill at intentional subtasks last, for these are metacognitive: they are not "learned" in the way that conventional subtasks are. It is true that writers can become comfortable about writing for a particular audience (say, teachers) about a particular topic (say "what I did last summer") for a particular purpose (to get an "A"). But writing situations are so varied and purposes so complex that we cannot be sure that writers will be able to handle situation Z just because they previously handled X and Y. In reviewing the reliable holistic scores of four essays written on four different topics by twenty-two college freshmen, Sarah Freedman and I found that fully one-quarter of the students wrote one essay with a score significantly higher or lower than the mean score of the other three essays. Further, we could not predict which essay would be anomalous. The effect of topic, then, is highly variable, as is the effect of genre.

The third category, mixed, is affected by the conventions of writing *and* by the intentions—if any—of the writer. Lexis, for instance, grows as children mature. Many word meanings stay constant over time; they are shared between the writer and any audience. On the other hand, a writer may consciously reject some words because an audience may not know or like them or use some because a particular topic demands them. Syntax also mixes convention and intention: students may be taught the conventional rules about how to make sentences complete; they may even speed their normal syntactic growth through sentence combining (Combs, 1976); however, older children decide how long, how varied, and how complex to make their sentences, depending on their audience and purpose (Crowhurst, 1977). Evidence shows that when students have difficulty writing to meet their intentions, their sentence structure and grammar suffer. Maimon and Nodine (1978) have found a significant reduction in the syntactic complexity of the writing of college freshmen when topics are more demanding.

Skilled writers can produce much better writing than unskilled writers not only because they have learned the conventions but because they have strategies for reducing the load on their attention. These strategies tell them when to plan and when to review their writing. In addition, skilled writers work longer than unskilled writers. Stallard (1974) found that a group of fifteen skilled twelfth-grade writers spent significantly more time on a given writing task than did a randomly selected group of fifteen twelfth-grade writers (a mean of 40.8 minutes compared to 22.6 minutes) but produced texts that were insignificantly longer (343 words compared to 309 words). Further, the skilled writers spent significantly more time in prewriting (a mean of 4.18 minutes compared to 1.20 minutes) and in rereading and revising (making 184 revisions to the random group's 64). The number of graphical revisions did not differ significantly between the two groups, nor did the number of syntactic revisions; however, the skilled writers made significantly more organizational (formal) and word choice (lexical) changes. These data suggest that twelfth-graders who are not classed as skilled writers lack a sophisticated strategy of revision: they correct graphical problems but do not spend the time to evaluate their writing against their purpose and intended meaning (topic). In fact, as the prewriting times suggest, the random group barely considered purpose and topic at all.

Revising: Conventions and Intentions

Stallard's evidence implies two kinds of revising: revising to fit conventions and revising to fit intentions. The first—often called editing or proofreading—occurs when writers are working on conventional or mixed subtasks. In conventional revising the writer matches the text against accepted rules of handwriting, spelling, punctuation, usage, grammar, and vocabulary—rules usually retrieved from memory. Young children and older but immature writers can revise this way because they can test their writing against memorized rules.

I do not mean to imply, however, that because immature writers *can* revise conventions they do so spontaneously. Evidence, both anecdotal and experimental, contradicts this hypothesis. Instead, unskilled writers tend to treat writing like speech. In speech, one muddles along, talking without much conscious planning. If an utterance—no matter how incoherent or ungrammatical—is interpreted by the listener, it is not usually repeated. Similarly, the unskilled writer forges ahead with writing as with speech, not looking back even though he or she lacks the immediate feedback of a listener. Even adult beginning writers must be required to review their writing: they do not naturally do so. Consider these examples (Shaughnessy, 1977) of the writing of a student in her late teens enrolled in a basic writing course at the City University of New York.

> *Passage written early in semester*
> Yesterday I saw something horrible. As I was walking down

the street. I saw a man and his dog. Though this was a
average man and his dog. This was a man beating his dog
to death. Which made me sick. I scream for him to stop,
Though I didnt get any answer from the man.

Passage written one month later

. . . The first assignment we had was a writing assignment. I
made so many mistakes that it was truly ridiculous. The
teacher returned my paper for me to correct it. The teacher
helped me correct it and find the reasons why I made the
mistakes.

　　The second writing assignment we had was a little more
difficult. I had my heart in this assignment not to make any
mistakes, but I was wrong. I made fewer mistakes but they
were there. This time I had to find them myself and understand why I made them. I found most of them but I really
couldn't understand how I made such idiotic mistakes. This
is where proof reading comes in. If I had proof read my
papers there wouldn't have been that many mistakes. (p. 277)

Shaughnessy adds, "In all such before-and-after examples, the
'after' samples bear many marks of revision (crossed-out words,
corrected punctuation, etc.), suggesting that the students have
acquired the important habit of going back over their sentences
with an eye to correctness" (p. 277). Elsewhere in her second
essay the student quoted above exults in her "new technique,"
which, she contends, has made her "the smartest girl in the
class." What she has learned is a strategy for compensating for
her lack of practice in all the subtasks. She does not have to produce language perfectly on the first try if she goes back to reread
and correct. In fact, her writing is better when she does *not* attend
much to conventional subtasks during her first draft. She is better
advised to attend in her first draft to intentional and mixed
subtasks.

　　Compared to revising to fit conventions, revising to fit intentions is much more complex. While revising to fit conventions,
writers match their texts against formal rules; in revising to fit
intentions, however, they must match their texts against decisions they made while forming their intentions. If they have no
intentions, they have nothing against which to evaluate their
writing. If they *have* intentions, writers ask: Does this text serve
my purpose? Does it reflect my meaning? Does it fulfill the needs
of my audience?

　　Even when writers consciously decide how to fulfill their intentions, they have difficulty deciding when their writing is good
enough. Without trying out their texts on the intended audience,
they are uncertain, for instance, about how much explanation a
particular concept demands. They have difficulty determining the

subtopics that would most interest their audience. In addition, they have trouble determining what tone to adopt in order to convince an audience.

Similar problems arise with meaning: writing often shakes intended meaning off its moorings. Expressed in writing, ideas that first seemed self-evident now seem shoddy. College students often complain that as they write, their intentions about meaning change and the end of their first draft often contradicts the beginning. In addition, writers are often frustrated with the inadequacy of words or syntax to carry subtle distinctions. While some writers sense when a text is "right," others are aware of the discrepancies between text and intended meaning but not skilled enough to resolve them.

Implications for Teaching

Probably the most important implication of this discussion is that writing can be taught to unskilled older students (who have other metacognitive abilities) far more efficiently than it can be taught to young children, who have very few metacognitive abilities. Because older students can be taught to apply attention-saving strategies like reviewing, they can complete subtasks successfully, even if they haven't learned them well. All they need is extra time. Shaughnessy's student illustrates this point.

But teaching students strategies does not excuse us from teaching them skills. Drill and practice are important for the novice—both adult and child; however, as Haynes (1978) explains, drill and practice cannot immediately improve the first drafts written by inexperienced writers. For example, even when novices spell words correctly on spelling tests—spending all their attention on spelling—they are likely to misspell the same words in first drafts. The lack of carry-over comes because their attention must be spent on other kinds of subtasks necessary to produce coherent writing. The benefits of drill and practice appear more readily in revising to fit conventions, a task that can be accomplished by students who have only rudimentary metacognitive skills. Revising to fit conventions—encouraged as a *normal* part of the writing process and not as a punishment for incompetence—frees students of their unreasonable expectations that their first drafts will be perfect. With practice, they may have the satisfaction of finding that they spend less time revising for conventions.

After older students have a rudimentary control of conventions, they should begin to focus on intentions. They should be reminded of the need to plan—to decide about their intentions—and taught to revise with these intentions in mind. Other strategies like prewriting heuristics can be taught at this stage (Young, 1976). Instead of drill and practice on conventions, their time can be well spent in sentence-combining exercises to increase their syntactic options (Combs, 1976). They need instruction about options in syntax, word choice, and organization in order to apply their decisions about purpose, audience, and topic in revising their drafts.

But strategies for revising to fit either conventions or intentions cannot be efficiently learned by students if the *instructor* corrects their drafts or if instructions for revision are vague. Studies have shown that mere quantity of corrections is uncorrelated with improvement in writing skills (Buxton, 1958; Clark, 1968). As for the quality of instructions, a small number of studies with children have shown that when given value indications about the faultiness of their messages ("I didn't understand"), young children very seldom improved them. They either repeated them or fell silent. When given more explicit indications about a message's inadequacy, however, even young children responded with improved messages (Glucksberg, Krauss, and Higgins, 1975). As the quality of instruction improves, so should the quality of student writing.

In order to teach the writing process, teachers must move from judging finished drafts to facilitating the writing and revising of various drafts of the same paper—particularly with students who have not mastered all of the subtasks. To teach best, teachers must understand the writing process as a complex whole with irregular patterns of growth and consolidation. Above all, they must stop regarding a draft-in-progress as an abomination to be "corrected." The writing of people in the "real world" is regularly criticized by their colleagues: read the acknowledgements that begin a book. Similarly, teachers can be their students' most influential colleagues, but only if teachers accept the responsibility of being clear, concise, and orderly in their writing assignments and in their responses to those assignments.

References

Bates, E. *Language and context: studies in the acquisition of pragmatics.* Unpublished doctoral dissertation, University of Chicago, 1974.

Buxton, E. W. *An experiment to test the effects of writing frequency and guided practice upon students' skill in written composition.* Unpublished doctoral dissertation, Stanford University, 1958.

Clark, W. G. *Evaluation of two techniques of teaching freshman composition: a final report.* Colorado Springs: U.S. Air Force Academy, 1968. (ERIC Document Reproduction Service No. ED 053 371).

Combs, W. E. Further effects of sentence-combining practice on writing ability. *Research in the Teaching of English,* 1976, *10,* 137–149.

Cooper, R. J., and Flavell, J. H. *Cognitive correlates of children's role-taking behavior.* Mimeographed copy, University of Minnesota, 1972.

Crowhurst, M. *Audience and mode of discourse effects on syntactic complexity at two grade levels.* Unpublished doctoral dissertation, University of Minnesota, 1977.

Flavell, J. H. *Cognitive development.* Englewood Cliffs, N.J.: Prentice-Hall, 1977.

Flavell, J. H., Friedrichs, A. G., and Hoyt, J. D. Developmental changes in memorization processes. *Cognitive Psychology,* 1970, *1,* 324–340.

Flavell, J. H., Botkin, P. I., Fry, C. L., Jr., Wright, J. W., and Jarvis, P. E. *The development of role-taking and communication skills in children.* New York: Wiley, 1968; reprinted by Krieger, 1975.

Flower, L. Writer-based prose. *College English,* 1979, *41,* 19–37.

Glucksberg, S., Krauss, R., and Higgins, E. T. The development of referential communication skills. *Review of Child Development Research,* 1975, *4,* 305–345.

Haynes, E. Using research in preparing to teach writing. *English Journal,* 1978, *67,* 82–88.

Kintsch, W. *The representation of meaning in memory.* Englewood Cliffs, N.J.: Lawrence Erlbaum Associates, 1975.

Maimon, E., and Nodine, B. Measuring syntactic growth: errors and expectations in sentence-combining practice with college freshmen. *Research in the Teaching of English,* 1978, *12,* 233–244.

Markman, E. Realizing you don't understand: a preliminary investigation. *Child Development,* 1977, *48,* 986–992.

Miller, G. A. The magical number seven, plus or minus two: some limits on our capacity for processing information. *Psychological Review,* 1956, *63,* 81–96. Reprinted in *The psychology of communication,* Baltimore, Md.: Penguin Books, 1967.

Robinson, E. J., and Robinson, W. P. Children's explanations of communication failure and the inadequacy of the misunderstood message. *Developmental Psychology,* 1977, *13,* 156–161.

Scardamalia, M., Bereiter, C., and McDonald, J. Roletaking in written communication investigated by manipulating anticipatory knowledge. Photocopy, York University, 1977. (ERIC Document Reproduction Service No. ED 151 792).

Shatz, M. The relationship between cognitive processes and the development of communication skills. In B. Keasey (Ed.), *Nebraska Symposium on Motivation.* Lincoln: University of Nebraska Press, 1978.

Shaughnessy, M. P. *Errors and expectations: a guide for the teacher of basic writing.* New York: Oxford University Press, 1977.

Stallard, C. K. An analysis of the writing behavior of good student writers. *Research in the Teaching of English,* 1974, *8,* 206-218.

Werner, H., and Kaplan, E. The development of word meaning through verbal context: an experimental study. *Journal of Psychology,* 1950, *29,* 251-257.

Whitehurst, G. The development of communication: changes with age and modeling. *Child Development,* 1976, *47,* 473-482.

Young, R. E. Invention. In G. Tate (Ed.), *Teaching composition: ten bibliographic essays.* Fort Worth: Texas Christian University Press, 1976.

A History of Revision: Theory versus Practice

Karen Hodges
University of Arkansas

After Charles Lamb had seen the authorial revisions of Milton's "Lycidas," he wrote:

> I had thought of the Lycidas as of a full-grown beauty—as springing up with all its parts absolute—till, in an evil hour, I was shown the original copy of it, together with the other minor poems of its author, in the library of Trinity, kept like some treasure, to be proud of. I wish they had thrown them in the Cam, or sent them after the latter Cantos of Spenser, into the Irish Channel. How it staggered me to see the fine things in their ore! interlined, corrected! as if their words were mortal, alterable, displaceable at pleasure! as if they might have been otherwise, and just as good! as if inspirations were made up of parts, and these fluctuating, successive, indifferent! I will never go into the workshop of any great artist again.[1]

Lamb's dismay over Milton's revisions reflects the characteristic nineteenth-century literary tenet that writing is inspired, not belabored; is produced as a whole, not by parts; and is immortal, hence neither "alterable" nor "displaceable." Thus Sir Walter Scott, Lamb's contemporary, had a reputation of writing in a veritable frenzy, of dashing off pages of perfect prose. A young lawyer who watched Scott at work exclaimed in awe:

> I have been watching it—it fascinates my eye—it never stops—page after page is finished and thrown on that heap of MS., and still it goes on unwearied—and so it will be till candles are brought in, and God knows how long after that. It is the same every night. . . .[2]

Similarly, John Cross, then George Eliot's husband, reported, "She told me that, in all that she considered her best writing, there was a 'not herself' which took possession of her."[3] Eliot's publisher seemed to concur about the lack of revision, for John Blackwood observed, "It [what Eliot is going to write] 'simmers'

24

in her mind as she says and then when she puts it upon paper it seems to pass into reality not to be altered."[4]

For these nineteenth-century writers, creation may have begun in the subconscious, but they mined their "ore," then "interlined" and "corrected" it just as John Milton did. Scott, for example, habitually composed three or four pages of his current novel, then "made corrections and additions . . . on the blank versos of the preceding leaves"; furthermore, he used his author proofs as a deliberate stage in the composing process, both following his editor's suggestions and making extensive changes of his own.[5] George Eliot's method of writing *Middlemarch,* despite her statements on the writing process, was to outline the novel part by part in a notebook and to make extensive revisions both of plan and parts.[6] This interesting discrepancy between stated theory and practice reflects the historical split between the content and form of writing and the present split between the revising and editing of writing (process re-visioned versus product corrected). To determine the causes of this disparity is to survey the history of rhetorical theory and writing practices.

To begin where one usually begins in matters of rhetoric—with Aristotle—is to discover a telling point: Aristotle is as silent on the topic of revision as writers in the nineteenth century preferred to be. Two probable reasons for this silence seem pertinent here. One, the ancient Greeks had no word for *composition* in the holistic, organic sense in which we use the term today; instead, the term referred to the skillful ordering of carefully selected sentence elements. In the *Rhetoric,* Aristotle writes,

> The foundation of good style is correctness of language which falls under five heads. (1) First, the proper use of connecting words, and the arrangement of them in the natural sequence. . . . (2) The second lies in calling things by their own special names and not by vague general ones. (3) The third is to avoid ambiguities. . . . (4) A fourth rule is to observe Protagoras' classification of nouns into male, female, and inanimate. . . . (5) A fifth rule is to express plurality, fewness, and unity by correct wording.[7]

Two, it is obvious that by *heuresis* Aristotle meant "finding" rather than "creating," choosing from a stock list of alternatives rather than being inspired by the muses:

> We now come to the Enthymemes, and will begin the subject with some general consideration of the *proper* way of *looking for* them, and then proceed to what is a distinct question, the lines of argument [topics] to be *embodied in* them [italics mine].[8]

The implications of these statements for the history of writing theory are clear. Alterations Aristotle relegates to the sentence level, to the editing of *forms* and their arrangement—in terms of the modern classroom, to the corrections of infelicities in usage, diction, and sentence structure. Moreover, his de-emphasis of the creative imagination leaves little room for the notion of re-visioning the whole. Composing in Aristotelean terms is to *find* and to structure content, and then to polish the product at the sentence level.

More directly influential than Aristotle on modern handbooks and methods of teaching writing is the Roman rhetorician Quintilian.[9] The major assimilator of the classical theories of rhetoric, Quintilian comments in his *Institutes of Oratory* on both editing and revising (although he does not so label his statements). He obviously recognizes the importance of editing when he observes "that the pen is not least serviceable when it is used to erase. Of correction there are three ways, to *add,* to *take away,* and to *alter.*"[10] It is this correlation between editing and "correction" that has defined the role of writer-as-editor in the history of composition—in short, an emphasis on linguistic propriety. In contrast to this dubious legacy, Quintilian illustrates in his own words that his comment on erasure has perhaps been construed too narrowly:

> But if by chance, while we are speaking, some glowing thought, suggested on the instant, should spring up in our minds, we must certainly not adhere too superstitiously to that which we have studied; for what we meditate is not to be settled with such nicety, that room is not to be allowed for a happy conception of the moment, when thoughts that suddenly arise in our minds are often inserted even in our written compositions. Hence the whole of this kind of exercise must be so ordered that we may easily depart from what we have arranged and easily return to it; since, though it is of the first importance to bring with us from home a prepared and precise array of language, yet it would be the greatest folly to reject the offerings of the moment.[11]

Here is evidence, then, of revision equated with re-visioning, a "glowing thought" during the composing process. Here is also a classical rhetorician's admonition that the writer/orator be flexible enough to incorporate such creative insights *during* the composing process. Not to do so, says Quintilian, "would be the greatest folly."

And yet the succeeding history of rhetorical theory is filled with examples of this folly, of the emphasis on correction of the product without Quintilian's correlating emphasis on revision of the process. The major causes of this narrowed approach to improving writing were not only the further separation of invention from style (or content from form) but the de-emphasis of invention: style (improving a product by correcting, adding, deleting, and rearranging words) became the focus. *Compositio,* then, during the medieval period as in Aristotle's time, was conceived of in the narrow sense of the rhythmic arrangement of well-chosen words—this narrowness further emphasized by the loss of the potential intellectual vitality of invention. The following comment, attributed to Bede, illustrates both the emphasis on correctness and the narrowed definition of rhetoric:

> The order of learning is as follows. Since *eloquentia* is the instrument of all teaching, they [the students] are instructed in it first. Its three parts are correct writing and correct delivery of what is written; proof of what is to be proved, which *dialectica* [logic] teaches; figures of words and sentences, which *rhetorica* hands down.[12]

There is no place in this schema for revision. Medieval students, in fact, spent a great deal of their time imitating classical works, both prose and poetry, not inventing forms of their own; thus they had no opportunity to reconsider or refocus. The changes that they made in their writing were surface editings, albeit extensive ones, designed to fulfill successfully the dictum that "*compositio* is [sentence] order polished smooth,"[13] or as C. S. Baldwin put it in his *Medieval Rhetoric and Poetic,* "Revision to this end involves the meticulous adjustment to tongue and ear."[14]

Medieval rhetoric found its home more in the pulpit than in the court of law; thus the influence of St. Augustine on the practical application of rhetorical theory is pervasive and significant. An examination of *De Doctrina Christiana, Book IV,* which deals with the style of preaching, shows that Augustine learned his school lessons well. He emphasizes correctness in grammar and clarity in diction, noting that "the function of grammar is traditionally to impart correctness of speech"; "if he [the speaker] can find correct words that are understood, he will choose these." And Augustine went on to advise the neophyte seminarian not "to spend his time on teachers of the art of rhetoric" but on "read[ing] or hear[ing] the eloquent and imitat[ing] them by practise."[15] Here again correction and imitation are emphasized rather than revision and invention.

With the Renaissance, and its revival of interest in classical literature, came an initial rebroadening of the definition of rhet-

oric. Appropriately, Quintilian was "rediscovered" in 1416 by the
Florentine Poggio Bracciolini, who unearthed a complete manuscript of the *Institutes of Oratory* from a monastery dungeon; by
1600, 118 editions of the work had spread their influence through
western Europe and England. Another humanist rhetorician who
exhibited conceptual breadth and exerted considerable influence
on early Renaissance rhetorical theory was Erasmus. His *De
Ratione Studii,* for example, promotes several pedagogical tenets
that are supportive of the process of revision. According to
Edward P. J. Corbett's summary, "He [Erasmus] . . . recommends
the exercise of . . . paraphrasing poetry into prose, and vice versa;
of rendering the same subject in two or more styles; of proving
a proposition along several different lines of argument; and of
construing from Latin into Greek."[16] Moreover, Erasmus' *De
Copia,* used widely as a rhetoric text in Tudor schools, emphasizes
achieving *copia,* or "fullness," in writing by generating a number
of ways of saying the same thing. Erasmus illustrates his point
in one place by listing two hundred variants of "Semper dum
vivam tui meminero."[17]

With Quintilian's "glowing thoughts" and Erasmus' copious
variants, the English Renaissance seemed disposed toward a full-
fledged theory of the place of revision in the composing process.
What resulted instead was a three-way split among rhetoricians
into Traditionalists, who followed classical theory; Ramists, who
again separated invention from style, relegating the former to the
study of logic and leaving only style as the province of rhetoric;
and Figurists, who concentrated on the surface features of style,
or schemes and tropes. Thus even the Traditionalists, those most
likely to have expanded on Quintilian and Erasmus, appear to
have been influenced by those—the Ramists and the Figurists—
whose approach to rhetoric was more exclusively connected with
surface features. Whatever the cause, their rhetorics deal with
what we would term editing, not revising.

A case in point is the Traditionalist Thomas Wilson, whose
The Arte of Rhetorique (1553) enjoyed wide popularity. Consider,
for example, his classical definition of *compositio* as the careful
arrangements of accurate wording: "when we have learned ac-
customable words to set forth our meaning we ought to joyne
them together in hearing the harmony. . . . Composition therefore
is an apt joyning together of wordes in such order, that neither
the eare shall espie an ierre, nor yet any man shall be dulled
with overlong drawing out of a sentence. . . ."[18] This *compositio*
Wilson cites as the major function of *Elocution,* or style, which

he considers the "most beautifull" part of rhetoric, the clothing "in Purple" of reason, which otherwise would appear "both bare and naked."[19] Elsewhere Wilson observes that "Rhetorike at large paintes well the cause."[20] Wilson's metaphors of clothing and paint point to a view of diction and syntax as surface dress; thus "correction" Wilson cites as a type of figure—the alteration of "a word or sentence, otherwise then we have spoken before, purposing thereby to augment the matter, and to make it appeare more vehement."[21] Obviously Wilson is speaking of stylistic editing, not holistic revision—of Quintilian's "erasure" rather than his "glowing thought."

Looking back on such statements from Renaissance rhetoricians, Francis Bacon spoke out in *The Advancement of Learning* against their preoccupation with style:

> Men began to hunt more after words than matter; and more after the choiceness of the phrase, and the round clean composition of the sentence, and the sweet falling of the clauses, and the varying and illustration of their works with tropes and figures, than after the weight of matter, worth of subject, soundness of argument, life of invention, or depth of judgment.[22]

What Bacon advocated instead as the primary function of rhetoric, again in *The Advancement,* "is to apply Reason to Imagination for the better moving of the Will." Or to cite Ben Jonson on the same topic, a man who aspires to write well must judge what he invents and order what he approves.[23]

These two seventeenth-century writers, especially Jonson, recognized the necessary interaction between invention (content) and style (form) and in so doing posed a holistic view of writing amenable to the idea of revision. To explore further Bacon's and Jonson's comments: if a writer stops in the process of composition to judge with reason what the imagination has discovered and arranges thereafter only that part of the content he or she has approved, considering too the ultimate purpose of the writing, then we have a rudimentary theory of revision—a process of selection, then a focusing reselection. Once again, however, the potential of revision narrowed to a concern with surface features. In the Renaissance, the narrowed focus of rhetoric resulted from a delight in words and in sentence rhythms; by the mid-seventeenth century, the same narrowing had, interestingly, recurred, but this time as a result of a growing emphasis on exactness and correctness (the influence of the roles of Reason and Will and the prelude to the early eighteenth century's fetish for linguistic propriety). The second half of the seventeenth century, then, became fairly well rule-bound in matters of writing. Students at Oxford and Cambridge, for example, trained in the arts of logic and rhetoric, learned "rules of clear thinking and correct expression" so that they could "apply them to the investigation and dissemination of the sciences."[24] When invention proceeds according to rules and expression becomes synonymous with correctness, there is, unfortunately, little place for Jonson's process of selection.

As if rule-bound invention and expression were not enough, the first half of the eighteenth century shares with the first decades of the twentieth century a nadir of rhetorical theory. Mere rules were not orderly enough; they had to be regularized. Centuries before, Quintilian had decried the grammarians for their "unpleasantly perverse attachment to exactness,"[25] adding that "it is one thing to speak Latin, and another to speak grammar."[26] The first part of the eighteenth century found writers in England speaking and writing "grammar" according to rigidly prescribed rules, the function of which was to purify the language and to ensure that people used it with a sameness of propriety and precision. In writing, therefore, the emphasis was on correctness; the result, according to Sterling Leonard, was a "conception of style—minutely logical, pure, precise, heavily formal, and circumlocutory";[27] a stereotyped, national expression that excluded a writer's personal signature and precipitated a scholar's warning that "if you must write like everybody else, it is useless to take up the pen."[28] This climate was obviously not conducive to notions of the place of revision in the writing process; writing was a product to be scrupulously combed for shibboleths, to be polished with the three p's of purity, propriety, and precision.

Fortunately for the history of rhetoric, rules for writing gave way to taste in writing in the latter half of the century. (Some rhetoricians, harbingers of early nineteenth-century romanticism, even went so far as to suggest that a student-writer discover an individual style.) The two most influential rhetoricians of this period were both Scotsmen, George Campbell (*The Philosophy of Rhetoric,* 1776) and Hugh Blair (*Lectures in Rhetoric and Belles Lettres,* 1783).

George Campbell's fascinating book is just what its title indicates—a *philosophy* of rhetoric; therefore, he explores human nature as well as rhetoric, specifically how the two illumine one another. As he says in his preface,

> It is his purpose in this Work, on the one hand, to exhibit, he does not say, a correct map, but a tolerable sketch of the human mind; and, aided by the lights which the Poet and the Orator so amply furnish, to disclose its secret movements, tracing its principal channels of perception and action, as near as possible, to their source: and, on the other hand, from the science of human nature, to ascertain with greater precision, the radical principles of that art, whose object it is, by the use of language, to operate on the soul of the hearer, in the way of informing, convincing, pleasing, moving, or persuading.[29]

In tracing the "principal channels" of the human mind, Campbell explores the causes of and relationships among sensations, memory, and imagination because it is these associations that produce the patterns that result in knowledge—and in the material of rhetoric. Campbell is especially interested in the mental patterns of resemblance (the mind associates ideas that are similar) and of causation (the mind seeks to understand the effect one concept or experience has on another) because both speaker and listener will follow this process in encoding and decoding material.

These are exciting ideas, ones that could form the basis for a very sophisticated theory of revision: the writer/speaker revises as he or she creates because the mind is continuously associating concepts in looking for a pattern, an ultimate focus. Moreover, since the mind of the reader/listener responds to the material in a similar way, the writer/speaker can revise the preliminary draft by whatever means will highlight these associations, hence "informing, convincing, pleasing, moving, or persuading" the audience. Unfortunately, Campbell never applied his philosophy in this way. A good deal of his work concerns ideas only; his application, some of Book II and Book III, ironically treats such topics as "grammatical purity," word choice, and word arrangement and includes an inordinately large section on sentence connectives. That Campbell so thoroughly divorced his theory from his application, so completely moved from process to product, is to be regretted.

Blair's *Lectures* are much less philosophically oriented: four are on taste, four on language (history of English), fifteen on style, ten on eloquence, and thirteen on the critical examination of "species of composition" (literary works).[30] His purpose is pragmatic: "next to speech, writing is beyond doubt, the most useful art which men possess." Blair's definition of taste centers on "delicacy" and "correctness" and his comments on style focus on the purity, propriety, and precision of words and on the precision, unity, strength, and harmony of "perfect" sentence structure. His observations, therefore, pertain to editing, not revising. From the *Lectures* it is obvious that Blair's classical mentor was Quintilian, but it is also obvious that his approach to his master was selective —unfortunately, since Blair has probably been the most influential rhetorician in American public schools.

Three quite disparate strands of writing theory wove through the nineteenth century. Blair and Campbell, joined by Richard Whately (*Elements of Rhetoric,* 1828), represent the "classical" strand. In addition, a "neoclassical" strand recurred, especially in the public schools, with heavy emphases on unity, coherence, usage, and grammar. Wordsworth became the spokesman for the third, the "romantic" strand, with his idea that writing overflows as powerful feelings recollected in moments of tranquility. As we have seen, Campbell's approach to writing points toward a process of revision, though he never follows through; the prescriptive approach allows no latitude for a theory of revision. Along with Quintilian, Erasmus, and Jonson, the Romantics quite possibly give us the best early theory of revision, despite the fact that for them spontaneity was synonymous with writing. They do so precisely because their emphasis is on the process, not the product, of writing. To summarize Wordsworth's now famous theory of writing: one has an experience (the heuristic for the resulting piece of writing), which one later recalls (selection of detail and focus) and gives form to (arrangement) through writing. Obviously for Wordsworth, the re-visioning occurs during the so-called prewriting stage: the initial experience is revised according to the details the mind chooses to remember and to emphasize. This theory had a tremendous impact on nineteenth-century writers of fiction as well as poetry: we have already noted George Eliot's claim that her ideas "simmered" before they found written form. But the impact was never felt in composition instruction in the public schools: at best, students read Blair and Whately; mostly they concentrated on grammar and usage and hence on editing written products.

The same three strands—classical, neoclassical, and romantic —have characterized twentieth-century writing instruction. By far the greatest influence has come from the neoclassical, the equating of composition with correctness. With the "rediscovery" of classical rhetoric, the classical strand has re-emerged, though for obvious reasons, such as the lack of a definitive theory, the emphasis has been on invention not revision. In sharp contrast to this classicism, the sixties offered a truncated version of the romantic impulse: write as you feel, with the emphasis on "over-flow," not on "recollection" with the selectivity that word connotes. We seem, then, to have made little headway, not only over the nineteenth century but since the time of Aristotle, in formulating a theory of what we know implicitly good writers do to become better—revise. Perhaps, then, we need to turn to the writers themselves for testimony—not of what they say they do (for some, like George Eliot, contradict themselves) but of what they actually do.

Let us return to the Renaissance, then, the first period in which we have access to multiple drafts of a single work that we know were produced by the same hand. Although a detailed analysis of the revision Sir Philip Sidney made of his *Arcadia* is beyond the scope of this paper,[31] a general assessment of the differences between the two versions is pertinent. The first version is a prose romance; the second, Sidney termed "an heroic poem in prose," a prose epic. In changing modes, as Hyder Rollins and Herschel Baker suggest, Sidney heightened the style appropriately and, using Virgil as his model, recast the straightforward narrative by inserting interpolated elements and increasing the thematic implications.[32] The result is a far different version of the "lost found," the basic archetypal plot with which Sidney was working. A series of specific incidents became a universal pattern, and the here-and-now of the popular romance was transformed into the there-and-beyond of the epic. These organic changes are vastly different from the stylistic editing Renaissance rhetoricians like Thomas Wilson spoke of, and one is reminded of Sidney's own words: "Only the poet, disdaining to be tied to any such subjection [the artificial rules of the grammarian], lifted up with the vigor of his own invention, doth grow in effect into another nature. . . ."[33]

Another transformed body of Renaissance literature is Michael Drayton's sonnet sequence first published in 1594 under the title *Ideas Mirrour, Amours in Quartorzains*. Between the 1594 and 1599 versions, as F. Y. St. Clair has pointed out, Drayton omitted twenty sonnets in the sequence, added twenty-eight new ones, reordered the retained sonnets, and edited extensively "to achieve a directness and concision" missing in the 1594 publication.[34] The most signficant evidence, however, that Drayton was revising (finding a new focus) lies in the differences between the controlling purposes and resulting voices of the two versions. He is the Petrarchan lyricist in the 1594 edition; and the mood of the sequence is the standard "sighs and tears." However, Drayton, like Sidney, "grow[s] in effect into another nature" for the 1599

edition: he will, I am again following St. Clair, "avoid lamenta-
tion" and "sing according to the mood of the moment and on a
variety of subjects."[35] In so doing Drayton becomes more the
philosopher-poet, a detached observer of what had once been his
own plight. The 1594 sonnett 33, for example, presents the standard Petrarchan tempest of sighs and tears over the standard
unrequited love. The poet is fearful and dying, his extreme emotional reaction both aided and reflected by abundant sighs and
flooding tears, which, in turn, reflect the vying of his heart and
eyes for the most dramatic expression of his grief. In sharp contrast, the 1599 revision does not even mention the woman who
had once caused this tumult, probably because Drayton is now
more interested in focusing on the absurdity of his heart and eyes
exchanging places ("mine eyes thus greedily doe gaze . . . Wishing
themselues that they were now my hart").[36] There is no emotional surfeit in the second version because reason interposes and
wit replaces tears; the re-visioning of the initial scene is complete.

Similar to Sidney's transformation of a prose romance into an
epic is Milton's revision of *Paradise Lost*. Again, the scope and
focus of this paper do not permit a detailed analysis of Milton's
revisions (as if the words of *Paradise Lost* "were mortal, alterable,
displaceable at pleasure!"), but a brief summary of the steps
Milton went through to achieve his masterpiece serves to emphasize that in the seventeenth as in the sixteenth century, the writer
became artist when he was able to expand his initial inspiration
through the process of extensive revision.[37] Initially *Paradise Lost*
was to have been a drama—the tragedy of Adam's fall—not an
epic. Milton sketched out five plans for the play, then extracted
and ordered materials from these drafts for his epic, adding, too,
ideas from still other sketches he had for additional tragedies,
such as *Adam in Banishment* and *The Flood*. Thereafter, the
apparent chronology of composition he followed was to add materials that would enlarge the scope of his work from drama to epic
—for example, enlarging the setting, Eden, to embrace heaven
and hell. This universal setting, in turn, transformed the tragedy
of Adam into the fall of man, a focus more fitting for an epic.
Even after Milton had revised drama into epic, he inserted completely new material, such as the buildng of Pandemonium (Book
I) and Satan's memorable encounter with Sin and Death (Book
II), as well as various philosophical passages more suitable for
epic than dramatic form. Thus while the rhetoricians of the late
seventeenth century were emphasizing exactness and correctness,
Milton was re-visioning the universe.

For another example of seventeenth-century revision, we can compare the manuscript with the published edition of George Herbert's "The Elixir."[38] What had been called "Perfection" in the original draft was retitled "The Elixir" in the final version to emphasize Herbert's revisioning of his poetic experience. Herbert amended his view that man's relationship with God is a state ("perfection") to a view that it is a transforming action that God inspires (thus God as "elixir"). This revised view of the relationship between God and man controls the other changes in the poem, including a deletion of a stanza, a reordering of two stanzas, and a complete rewriting of two more stanzas in this short (six-stanza) poem. With these extensive changes, the original, rather passive persona who wishes to be pleasing to God simply by "referr[ing] All Things" to Him becomes the revised, now active persona who wishes to *see* God in all things as well as to *do* things for Him. An altered stanza in the revised version elaborates on this point by stressing action guided by God Who can transform any activity into perfection ("Nothing can be so mean / Which with his tincture . . . / Will not grow bright and clean."). Aptly reflected in the rewriting of this poem is this thematic point that perfection *grows*: it is progression, not stasis. True, there are surface editings in the final version, but more significant is the revision that results from and reflects Herbert's altered vision of the relationship between God and man.

The succeeding Neoclassical Age is *the* age of editing, of surface polishing toward propriety and precision. No one was, or probably has been since, a more meticulous editor of his own work than Alexander Pope. Yet it would be a mistake to view Pope as a surface tinkerer only. His *Rape of the Lock* is a well-known case in point. Although the original poem was mock-heroic, it was not a mock-epic. As Sidney revised a romance into a prose epic and as Milton revised a tragedy into an epic, so Pope transformed an occasional poem into a broadened view of the follies and foibles of humankind. In doing so, he added all of the epic machinery—the sylphs who intervene in human affairs, the mock-epic battle of the card game, and the descent into the underworld (the visit to the Cave of Spleen).

An intriguing point emerges from this discussion of the revisions of Sidney, Milton, Drayton, and Pope. In each instance, the revision becomes a more generalized version of the original. The writer, understandably, gains distance on the material, and the result is more abstract and philosophical. Another illustration of this tendency is Samuel Richardson's seventh and final edition of

Pamela (1801). Almost as dedicated an editor as Pope, Richardson
tinkered with his novels continuously, even after they were published, but the final version of *Pamela* presents a completely re-
vamped heroine rather than an edited story.[39] In the 1801 edition,
a much refined "lady" Pamela supercedes her original (1741)
"country cousin"; the new Pamela is a woman much surer of
herself, more in control of her environment, and quite inclined
toward philosophical observations. The original Pamela meets
the "impudent gentleman" with a lack of assurance revealed in
her language—"I hope, said I"—and in her subsequent action of
tripping away as fast as she can. The revised Pamela, however,
is quite assertive: her vague "hope" becomes the definite "I will
add, returned I"; and rather than tripping, with all its nuances
of silly awkwardness, Pamela *snatches* her hand from the gentleman and hurries away. Immediately after her departure, the
original Pamela addresses her parents with "Why, dear Father
and Mother, to be sure he grows quite a rake!" A long paragraph
of similar exclamations follows, ending with Pamela shrieking,
"But, God bless me, say I, and send me out of this wicked house!"
Her revised counterpart would never shriek; instead of crying to
her parents, she turns philosopher and analyzes the man's character as a vile example of wicked folly. Most readers find the
original Pamela more charming, but obviously Richardson's view
both of her and of his novel's purpose had changed and produced
a substantial revision.

In contrast to the theoretical emphasis on editing as the control
of writing in the eighteenth century is the belief in the synonymy
of writing and inspiration in the nineteenth century. Writers,
however, proved a constant: just as the Neoclassicists revised and
edited inspiration, so did the Romantics. A striking example is the
series of drafts that Keats wrote in working toward a final version
of "The Eve of St. Agnes." (It is comforting, too, to realize that
Keats had great difficulty with spelling.) Figure 1 illustrates the
changes Keats made in stanza 24 as it underwent three revisions.

Again, these changes extend beyond surface editing. Keats is
seeking a thematic focus for the entire poem and finds it in this
stanza in the contrasts between the frozen art of the casement
window and the natural world it seeks to represent (fruits, flowers,
and grass; the tiger moth); more broadly, between death ("the
scutcheon blushd with Blood") and life. In his first try, the shift
from the vaguely described casement to Madeline kneeling be-
neath it does not convey this ultimate vision and controlling
focus. Keats may well have been inspired, but to him and despite
romantic theory, inspiration was hardly enough.

Another nineteenth-century writer who labored hard and long over his works was Edgar Allan Poe. Many of the changes are minor, especially clarifying corrections in punctuation and diction, changes in keeping with what one would expect of the meticulous editor that Poe was. An examination of the four variant texts of his "The Murders in the Rue Morgue," however, reveals a revision of purpose: a change from a detached study of analysis to an active demonstration of the workings of the imagination. In fact, the burden for solving the murders seems to shift from the detective Dupin to the reader. As Poe himself observed, "Where is the ingenuity of unravelling a web which you yourself (the author) have woven for the express purpose of unravelling?"[40] In his revision, therefore, Poe inserts false clues and deletes certain passages so that the reader, like a detective, works with frag-

Draft A

1   A Casement ~~ach'd~~ tripple archd and diamonded
2   With many coloured glass fronted the Moon
3   In midst ~~of which~~ ^{wereof} a shilded scutcheon shed
4   High blushing gules: ~~upon she kneeled saintly~~ down
5   And inly prayed for grace and heavenly boon
6   The blood red gules fell on her silver cross
7   And ~~her~~ white(est) hands devout

Draft B

1   ^{There was} A Casement tipple archd and high
2   All garlanded with carven imageries
3   Of fruits & ~~trailing~~ flowers and sunny corn _{ears parchd}

Draft C

1   A Casement high and tripple archd there was
2   All gardneded with carven imageries
3   Of fruits and flowers and bunches of knot grass;
4   And diamonded with panes of quaint device
5   Innumerable of stains and splendid dies

6   ^{sunset} ~~As is the wing of evening tiger moths;~~ (As is the tger moths ~~rich~~ deep ~~damasked~~ wjngs)
7   ~~And~~ in ~~the~~ midst 'momg ~~man~~ heraldries (^{whereft} ^{thousand})
8   And ~~dim twilight~~ twilight saints and dim emblasonings
9   A shielded scutcheon blushd with Blood of Queens & Kings

Figure 1. Three revisions of stanza 24 from "The Eve of St. Agnes." Adapted from Wright Thomas and Stuart Gerry Brown, *Reading Poems: An Introduction to Critical Study* (New York: Oxford University Press, 1941), p. 620. The manuscript is in the Widener Library at Harvard University.

mentary evidence. In the following sentence, for example, Poe added dashes to emphasize the chair (in the first version he merely used commas), no doubt so that the reader will believe the chair important in solving the mystery (it is not): "A heavy club of wood, or a broad bar of iron—a chair—any large, heavy, and obtuse weapon. . . ." Deleted information, like the red herring implicit in his use of dashes, imposes Poe's intent on the reader's imagination: "the fugitive's attention was arrested by a light [(the only one apparent except those of the town-lamps)] gleaming from the open window. . . ." By deleting the bracketed material in his revision, Poe again engaged the reader in the solving of the murders. "Why *that* light?" the reader-detective muses, not knowing it was the "only one."

Because many twentieth-century writers appear to enjoy talking about their creative revisions—and save their worksheets for proof —there are many examples to choose from in illustrating what currently goes on in the artist's workshop. As John Updike has said, "Writing and rewriting are a constant search for what one is saying."[41] This search was shared by William Faulkner, whose entire literary career seems to have been one of recycling: ideas become episodes; episodes, published stories; stories, refashioned parts of novels; novels, segments of a series of perspectives first on the Snopeses and Sartorises, then on the South, ultimately on human nature. Faulkner himself once described this process of re-visioning:

> When I began it [*The Hamlet*], it produced Spotted Horses, went no further. About two years later suddenly I had The Hound, then Jamshyd's Courtyard, mainly because Spotted Horses had created a character I fell in love with. . . .
> Meanwhile my book had created Snopes and his clan, who produced stories in their saga which are to fall in a larger volume. . . . This over about ten years, until one day I decided I had better start on the first volume or I'd never get any of it down. So I wrote an induction toward the spotted horse story, which included Barn Burning and Wash, which I discovered had no place in that book at all. Spotted horses became a larger story, picked up the Hound . . . and went on with Jamshyd's Courtyard.[42]

Faulkner's method here is very much like that which T. S. Eliot said produced "Ash Wednesday":

> Yes, like "The Hollow Men," it originated out of separate poems. . . . Then gradually I came to see it as a sequence. That's one way in which my mind does seem to have worked

> throughout the years poetically—doing things separately and
> then seeing the possibility of fusing them together, altering
> them, and making a kind of whole of them.[43]

Searching, gaining perspective, turning fragments into artistic wholes—these seem to form the message from the artist's workshop, lessons not emphasized in rhetorical theory and yet lessons we want our students not simply to learn but to experience. How do we emphasize this process of revision to them? Obviously, there exists no cohesive theory of revision to guide us, as there is with invention. Moreover, since revision is a process of discovery that appears to initiate with a "glowing thought," a comprehensive theory of revision awaits further work from neurobiologists on the mystery that is the human brain. Ultimately, we would like answers to such questions as what keys these glowing thoughts—word association? If so, is revision initially a right-brain function? If so, again, what implications does this have for our teaching of revision? Or, how does a successful writer know whether or not to pursue a glowing thought and how to integrate it, if he or she so chooses, into previous ideas?

These are thorny questions, but we need not wait for answers before we apply in the classroom what we know about revision—good writers have always revised to transform the adequate fragment into the excellent whole. I suggest, as a beginning, we revise Aristotle's notion of topics to "invent" our own "classical" theory of revision. Students then will have a heuristics of revision as well as of invention to stimulate their search for excellence.

Topics of Revision

1. Change point of view: within the discourse (a different "self" of the writer speaks) and outside the discourse (the "audience" of the original draft responds).
2. Change structure: move from inductive to deductive, for example, or from a unit structure to a norm method of development.
3. Change focus: select a small portion of the original as a new focus and expand.
4. Change tone: try a comic/satiric approach to a serious subject, for example.
5. Change purpose, such as "complaining" in the first draft, then persuading for change in the revision.
6. Change audience.

7. Change mode: if the original was a comparison/contrast of two people, for example, rework the discourse into a broader essay of classification, with the two people serving as examples of their respective categories.

8. Change genre: rather than an essay defining failure, for example, write a short story illustrating this trait.

9. Experiment with different "publishers": how would the language and format vary, for example, between writing an article on a women's football team for *Newsweek* and rewriting it for *Sports Illustrated* or *Psychology Today* or *Redbook?*

Notes

1. "Essays of Elia," in *Life and Works,* ed. Alfred Ainger (Troy, N.Y.: Lovell, Coryell, & Co., 1899), II: 300.

2. Cited in Philip Gaskell, *From Writer to Reader: Studies in Editorial Method* (Oxford: At the Clarendon Press, 1978), p. 101.

3. Cited in Jerome Beaty, *"Middlemarch" from Notebook to Novel: A Study of George Eliot's Creative Method.* Illinois Studies in Language and Literature, vol. 47 (Urbana: University of Illinois Press, 1960), p. 106.

4. Cited in Beaty, p. 107.

5. Gaskell, pp. 102-3.

6. This point is more fully made in Beaty's study.

7. Aristotle *Rhetoric* (trans. W. Rhys Roberts) 3. 5. 5.

8. *Rhetoric* 2. 21. 22.

9. See, for example, Donald Stewart, "The Legacy of Quintilian," *English Education* 11 (December 1979): 103-17.

10. Quintilian *Institutes of Oratory* (trans. John Selby Watson) 10. 4. 1.

11. *Institutes* 10. 6. 5.

12. Cited in Charles Sears Baldwin, *Medieval Rhetoric and Poetic: Interpreted from Representative Works* (New York: Macmillan Co., 1928), pp. 128-29.

13. From the *Candelabrum,* Book I, cited by Baldwin, p. 216.

14. Baldwin, p. 84.

15. Augustine *On Christian Doctrine* (trans. D. W. Robertson), sections 3, 5, 10.

16. Edward P. J. Corbett, *Classical Rhetoric for the Modern Student* (New York: Oxford University Press, 1965), p. 546.

17. Cited in Corbett, p. 547.

18. *Wilson's Art of Rhetorique,* ed. G. H. Mair (Oxford: At the Clarendon Press, 1909), p. 166.

19. Ibid., p. 160.

20. Ibid., p. xvi.

21. Ibid., p. 186.

22. Francis Bacon, *The Advancement of Learning,* ed. William A. Armstrong (London: Athlone Press, 1975), pp. 70–71.

23. Ben Jonson, *Timber,* in *The Renaissance in England: Non-dramatic Prose and Verse of the Sixteenth Century,* eds. Hyder E. Rollins and Herschel Baker (Boston: D. C. Heath & Co., 1954), p. 665.

24. John R. Mulder, *The Temple of the Mind: Education and Literary Taste in Seventeenth-Century England* (New York: Pegasus, 1969), p. 27.

25. *Institutes* 1. 6. 17.

26. *Institutes* 1. 6. 27.

27. Sterling Leonard, *The Doctrine of Correctness in English Usage, 1700–1800,* University of Wisconsin Studies in Language and Literature, no. 25 (Madison: University of Wisconsin Press, 1929), p. 238.

28. A. Albalat, *L'art d'écrire* (Colin, 1909), p. 57.

29. George Campbell, *The Philosophy of Rhetoric,* ed. Lloyd F. Bitzer (Carbondale and Edwardsville: Southern Illinois University Press, 1963), p. xliii.

30. As noted by Harold F. Harding, ed., *Lectures in Rhetoric and Belles Lettres,* by Hugh Blair (Carbondale and Edwardsville: Southern Illinois University Press, 1965), pp. xii–xiii.

31. For a full-length study, see R. W. Zandvoort, *Sidney's "Arcadia": A Comparison between the Two Versions* (Amsterdam: N. V. Swets and Zeitlinger, 1929).

32. Hyder E. Rollins and Herschel Baker, eds., *The Renaissance in England: Non-dramatic Prose and Verse of the Sixteenth Century* (Boston: D. C. Heath & Co., 1954), p. 737.

33. Sir Philip Sidney, *The Defense of Poesy,* in Rollins and Baker, p. 607.

34. F. Y. St. Clair, "Drayton's First Revision of His Sonnets," *Studies in Philology* 36 (1939): 44–45 and 48.

35. St. Clair, p. 49.

36. The texts for the two versions of sonnet 33 are found in St. Clair, p. 48.

37. I am indebted in this summary of Milton's revisions to Allan H. Gilbert, *On the Composition of "Paradise Lost": A Study of the Ordering and Insertion of Material* (New York: Octagon Books, 1966).

38. For the texts of the poem, see F. E. Hutchison, ed., *The Works of George Herbert* (Oxford: At the University Press, 1941), pp. 184–85. I am indebted especially to Charles Molesworth, "Herbert's 'The Elixir': Revision towards Action," *Concerning Poetry* 5 (Fall 1972): 12–20; see also Roger Fogleman, "Revision and Improvement in George Herbert's *The Temple,*" *Nassau Review* 5 (1969): 65–85.

39. I am indebted in the discussion that follows to Gaskell, pp. 63–79. The passages that I compare are reproduced on pp. 66–67.

40. Quoted in Joel Kenneth Asarch, "A Telling Tale: Poe's Revisions in 'The Murders in the Rue Morgue,'" *Library Chronicle* 41 (1976): 88.

Asarch offers a fuller treatment of Poe's revisions of this story and is
the source of my comments throughout this paragraph.

41. Quoted in Donald M. Murray, "Internal Revision: A Process of
Discovery," in *Research on Composing: Points of Departure,* eds.
Charles R. Cooper and Lee Odell (Urbana, Ill.: National Council of
Teachers of English, 1978), p. 103.

42. Malcolm Cowley, *The Faulkner-Cowley File: Letters and Memories, 1944-1962* (New York: Viking Press, 1966), pp. 25-26. There are
many book-length studies of Faulkner's revisions, for example, Joanne
V. Creighton, *William Faulkner's Craft of Revision* (Detroit: Wayne
State University Press, 1977); Gerald Langford, *Faulkner's Revisions of
"Absalom, Absalom!": A Collation of the Manuscript and the Printed
Book* (Austin: University of Texas Press, 1971); James Early, *The Making of "Go Down, Moses"* (Dallas: Southern Methodist University Press,
1972).

43. Quoted in George Plimpton, ed., *Writers at Work: The "Paris Review" Interviews,* second series (New York: Viking Press, 1963), p. 100.

H. G. Wells' *The Outline of History*: A Study in Revision

R. Baird Shuman
University of Illinois at Urbana-Champaign

Few books see the light of day that have not undergone countless revisions. Generally the writer revises the work several times before submitting it to a publisher. Ernest Hemingway, a disciplined literary artist who seldom missed a day of writing, set for himself the goal of producing 800 to 1,000 words daily and then of cutting this work to the bone, often to 100 words. An examination of his manuscripts reveals that Hemingway often cut beautiful and effective passages because they did not add to the muscularity and spareness that he was trying to achieve. His finished products are highly controlled, stringently disciplined. His sentences are often terse and uncomplicated. His vocabulary is simple and direct. His original pages reveal much longer, more convoluted sentences and a somewhat more esoteric vocabulary than readers find in his published short stories and novels.

In spite of the many revisions authors make, it is not uncommon for publishers to return promising manuscripts, agreeing to reconsider them if authors will carry out revisions suggested by the editor and by publishers' consultants, who review pieces submitted for publication. In some cases, suggested revisions are so extensive as to constitute a virtual rewriting of the work. Such was the case with Harper Lee's highly praised *To Kill a Mockingbird*; to get the manuscript into the form suggested by the publisher, Ms. Lee resigned from her job with an airline company and devoted a full year to extensive revision and rewriting.

For most authors, the revision process continues long after they have submitted their manuscripts for publication. When a manuscript is accepted for publication, the copy editor usually returns it to the author, who must approve the copy editing. At this stage, authors usually make further revisions, sometimes at the direction of the copy editor and sometimes on their own. The copy-edited typescript is then read again by the copy editor, who may make further changes before the manuscript is set in type.

43

When the manuscript has been typeset, long pages of galley proofs are produced. The copy editor then reads and often revises these and sends them on to the author for verification, and what publishers hope will be final revisions. Considerable revision may still take place at this stage, after which the book is set in page proof. The pages, numbered and looking very much as they will in the bound volume, again undergo several readings, and often further revisions are made, even though authors who demand extensive revisions at this point may themselves have to pay for the expense of resetting and renumbering the pages. The book that one sees as a bound volume is quite different indeed from the manuscript or typescript that left the author's hands.

For the purposes of this paper, I will focus on a highly competent stylist, H. G. Wells, who usually did not revise so fully as writers like Hemingway and Lee. Wells, in writing factual accounts of historical events in *The Outline of History,* was writing for a general but fairly well-educated audience. His accounts had to be accurate, on the one hand, in order that his credibility be unquestioned, and readable, on the other hand, in order that the interest of a general audience would be sustained. The portion of *Outline* to be considered here is the first two typescript pages of Chapter 24, "The Career of Alexander the Great." As one can see by looking at a reproduction of these two pages, which constitute two and one-half pages in the published volume, the revisions are substantial (Figure 1). The published text reveals that later revisions were made, perhaps in galley proofs by the author himself or at some other stage by Wells' editor.

You will note that Wells initially entitled Chapter 24 "Alexander the Great," a title that suggests a broader biographical treatment than the author could be expected to give in thirty-four pages. In changing the title to "The Career of Alexander the Great," Wells narrows the topic somewhat and is also more descriptive. The revision imposes a limitation on the subject matter, albeit not a very extensive one. It also sharpens the focus of the chapter.

Moving into the chapter itself, Wells again limited a statement that in its original expression—"all the greatness"—was somewhat immoderate, too all-inclusive. Wells was undoubetdly aware that any statement including the word *all* must be scrutinized carefully to determine whether it holds together logically. To say "All of the diners in the restaurant ordered soup" may be demonstrably true. To say, on the other hand, that Philip planned *all* of the greatness that his son achieved is clearly fallacious because Philip could not have anticipated *all* of his son's accomplishments. The substitution of "much of" makes the statement acceptable logically by moving from the all-proposition of formal logic to the some-proposition.

With the insertion of "who," Wells made "laid the foundations" and "had indeed already begun" parallel with "who planned." The original rendering was not incorrect; however, the revision solidifies and strengthens the expository fabric of the sentence, giving a unity and coherence to Philip's actions, as it were. In the same sentence, by changing "weapons" to "tools," broadening the term from a specific kind of tool to tools in general, Wells achieves greater accuracy. Both words are used metaphorically, but the more general word is preferable to the specific one because it extends the metaphor.

In omitting almost two lines and replacing them with "at the time of his death," Wells shows good judgment. In the original he told too much and in so doing, even though what he said was factually correct, he had allowed himself to digress. He was diverting the reader's attention from the matter at hand—the career of Alexander the Great—and presenting unnecessary biographical information. Even though Wells, having researched his topic competently, might know all manner of factual information about Alexander, right down to the name of his dog or his preference in salad dressings, such information would not likely shed light on Alexander's career, the stated topic of the chapter.

Having revised the preceding sentence to achieve parallel structure, Wells must then revise the initial pronoun in the following sentence. Before the revision, the pronoun *he* of the next sentence quite clearly referred to Philip; with the revision, the reference is not quite so clear, so Philip's name was reintroduced —not in the manuscript revision shown in Figure 1 but in the final printed version of *The Outline of History* (New York: Macmillan Co., 1920).

Speaking of Philip's greatness, Wells wrote, ". . . he was mot [not] simply a man of the utmost intelligence and ability but his range of ideas. . . ." The version printed in 1920 reads, ". . . he was a man of the utmost intelligence and ability, and his range of ideas. . . ." Either Wells or his copy editor decided quite astutely that the negation, *not simply,* detracted from the assertion of Philip's greatness. The phrase, easily dropped from the sentence, affects, however, the coordinating conjunction, *but.* The term *not simply* is a variant of *not only,* which is in standard English followed by the correlative term, *but also*; in Wells' original, the correlative term is used elliptically. When the first element is dropped, however, the second element must be replaced by the coordinating conjunction, *and.*

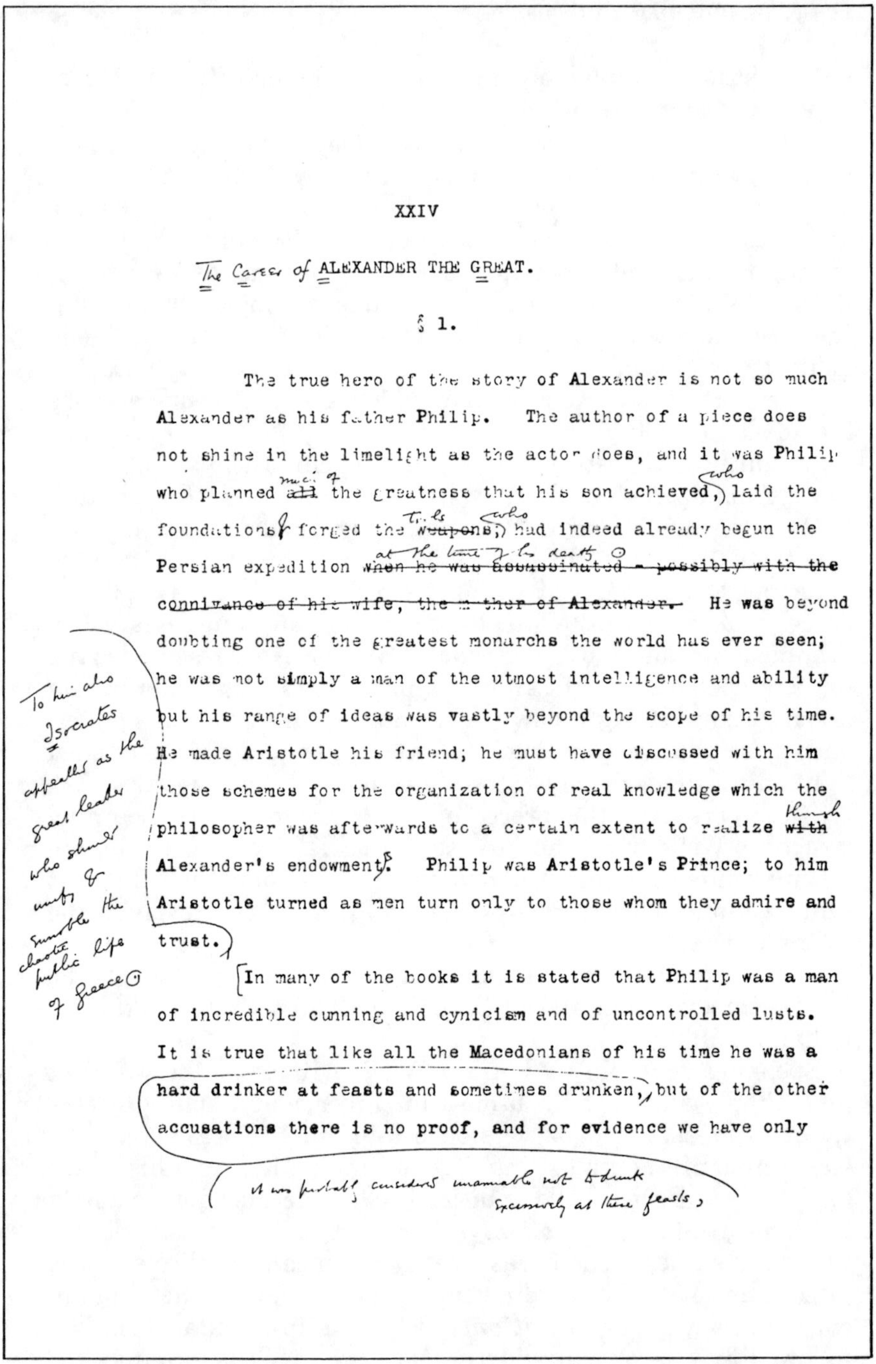

The Career of ALEXANDER THE GREAT.

§ 1.

The true hero of the story of Alexander is not so much Alexander as his father Philip. The author of a piece does not shine in the limelight as the actor does, and it was Philip who planned ~~all~~ *much of* the greatness that his son achieved, *who* laid the foundations, forged the ~~weapons~~ *Tools* *who* had indeed already begun the Persian expedition ~~when he was assassinated - possibly with the connivance of his wife, the mother of Alexander.~~ *at the time of his death* He was beyond doubting one of the greatest monarchs the world has ever seen; he was not simply a man of the utmost intelligence and ability but his range of ideas was vastly beyond the scope of his time. He made Aristotle his friend; he must have discussed with him those schemes for the organization of real knowledge which the philosopher was afterwards to a certain extent to realize ~~with~~ *through* Alexander's endowment. Philip was Aristotle's Prince; to him Aristotle turned as men turn only to those whom they admire and trust.

To him also Isocrates appealed as the great leader who should & unify the chaotic public life of Greece

[In many of the books it is stated that Philip was a man of incredible cunning and cynicism and of uncontrolled lusts. It is true that like all the Macedonians of his time he was a hard drinker at feasts and sometimes drunken, but of the other accusations there is no proof, and for evidence we have only

It was probably considered unmannerly not to drink excessively at these feasts,

Figure 1. First two typescript pages of chapter 24, "The Career of Alexander the Great." The typescript of H. G. Wells' *The Outline of History* is housed in the

the railings of such antagonists as Demosthenes, the Athenian

provably

Illus. demagogue and orator, a man ~~possibly~~ a rhetorical liar. ~~This~~ *a quotation*

will serve to show

~~was~~ the style of his attacks. It is from one of his **Phillipics**

as his masterpieces of abuse directed against Philip are called:

"Philip - a man who not only is no Greek, and no way akin
to the Greeks, but is not even a barbarian from a respect-
table country - no, a pestilent fellow of Macedon, a country from which we never get even a decent slave."

And so on and so on. Some of this Athenian's gutter

(for gutter mud this is)

mud) still sticks to the name of Philip.

[When Philip became king of Macedonia in 359 B.C., his

country was a little country without a sea-port or industries

or any considerable city. It had a sturdy peasant population,

(almost

Greek) in language and ready to be Greek in sympathies, but more

purely Nordic in blood than any people to the south of it. ~~He~~ *Philip*

made this little state into a great one; he created the most

efficient

Illus. ~~official~~ military organization the world had so far seen, and

he had got most of Greece into one confederacy under his **leader**-

ship at the time of his death. And his extraordinary quality,

his power of thinking out beyond the current ideas of his time,

but so much in these matters as

is shown ~~in nothing more plainly than~~ in the care with which he

had his son trained to carry on the policy he had created. ~~A~~

Alexander was, as few other monarchs have ever been, a specially

(but

educated king, he was educated for empire. Aristotle was) one

(able

of the several) tutors his father chose for him. Philip confi-

ded his policy to him, and entrusted him with commands and

authority by the time he was sixteen. He commanded the **cavalry**

at Chaeronea under his father's eye. He was nursed into power

- generously and unsuspiciously. [To anyone who reads his **life**

with care it is evident that **Alexander** started with an equipment

of training and ideas of unprecedented value. As he got beyond

the wisdom of his upbringing he began to blunder and behave ——

sometimes with a dreadful folly. The defects of his charac-

ter were triumphant over his upbringing long before he died.

Not exempt from the awkward wordiness that reduces the effectiveness of any writing, Wells wrote, ". . . which the philosopher was afterwards to a certain extent to realize through Alexander's endowments." This sentence is a blunderbuss. It lumbers. It lacks grace. Somewhere in the editing process before the 1920 edition, the rendering mercifully becomes, ". . . which the philosopher was to realize later through Alexander's endowments." A yet more graceful rendition would place *later* before the infinitive: "later to realize."

Caution dictated the next variance between Wells' typescript and the printed text. Wells first wrote simply, "Philip was Aristotle's Prince." This bald statement is made considerably more tentative in the 1920 edition: "Philip, so far as we can judge, seems to have been Aristotle's 'Prince.'" Note that the simple copulative *was* not only becomes the tentative *seems* but also is hedged by "so far as we can judge." Stylistically, the original sentence is preferable; however, the more cautious revision is more accurate. Wells also lent credibility to his claim by inserting a second example (see his marginal note in Figure 1), showing in this case that Isocrates, perhaps the greatest historian of his age and one of the greatest Greek orators, acknowledged Philip's greatness also.

Wells' second paragraph, following one of high praise, seeks to strike an objective balance—or at least to woo its readers into thinking that one has been achieved. Wells, however, is clearly Philip's defender, for in pointing out that Philip was thought to be a man of "incredible cunning and cynicism and of uncontrolled lusts," he sees fit to add in the lower margin the moderating statement, "it was probably considered unamiable not to drink excessively at these [the word *these* is omitted from the 1920 version] feasts."

The rather awkward usage *of the* ("in many of the books") is omitted in the 1920 edition; instead, we find "in many books." Also omitted is the reference to Philip's alleged cunning; presumably Wells or his editors thought that cynicism and uncontrolled lust were a sufficient counterbalance to the accolade that Wells heaped upon Philip in the first paragraph. For purely stylistic reasons, the printed version reads, "It is true that at feasts [moved up from the following line of the typescript], like all Macedonians of his time [,] he was a hard drinker and sometimes drunken. . . ." Apparently the *all* in this passage, even though demonstrably untrue, one would think, did not bother Wells or his editors. The statement is made with rather a flourish and is not meant to be taken in a wholly serious way. However, the next clause of the sentence, "but of the other accusations there is no proof," is moderated in the 1920 edition to read "there is no *real* proof [my italics]."

If Wells is biased in Philip's favor, he is equally biased against Demosthenes, the famed orator, who was one of Philip's detractors. He begins by calling him "possibly a rhetorical liar," moving one notch closer to certitude by revising *possibly* to *probably*. In the 1920 edition, however, his immoderate statement becomes "a man of reckless rhetoric." This alliterative statement, while seemingly less vehement than the original, is perhaps in subtle ways actually more vehement because it leaves more to the reader's imagination. The following passage, reproduced here in its revised manuscript form is again altered in the 1920 edition.

> *Revised typescript*
> A quotation will serve to show the style of his attacks. It is from one of his *Phillipics* [*sic*] as his masterpieces of abuse directed against Philip are called:
> *Published version*
> The quotation of a phrase or so will serve to show to what the patriotic anger of Demosthenes could bring him. In one of the *Philippics,* as his denunciations of Philip are called, he gives vent in this style:

Note the increased specificity of the published version. The quite disparaging "abuse" is moderated in tone—without changing the impact substantially—to "gives vent in this style."

Wells' contempt for Demosthenes spilled out further in the next sentence, which is given in its revised typescript form side by side with the version published in 1920.

> *Revised typescript*
> Some of the Athenian's gutter mud, for gutter mud this is, still sticks to the name of Philip.
> *Published version*
> We know, as a matter of fact, that the Macedonians were an Aryan people very closely akin to the Greeks, and that Philip was probably the best educated man of his time. This was the spirit in which the adverse accounts of Philip were written.

The expanded version elevates the presentation while supplying additional factual information. The earlier version is personally vindictive, focusing on Demosthenes; the published version, by focusing on Philip, makes its point while simultaneously moving forward the factual presentation of the account.

The paragraph that follows might have been strengthened had the repetition of *country* been avoided: "his country was a little country." However, what follows is pleasingly parallel, almost melodic: "without a sea-port or industries or any considerable city." The unsophistication of this series stylistically parallels the unsophistication of Philip's Macedonia and is wholly appropriate to what is being said. The style suits the sense, the sense the style.

Realizing that at the time the Macedonians spoke a patois and were not linguistically comparable to the Athenians, Wells tempered his statement that the population of Macedonia was "Greek in language" to "Greek *almost* in language [my italics]." The more usual position for *almost* would have been before *Greek*; it served Wells' artistic purposes better, nevertheless, to place the qualifier after the proper noun, placing the emphasis of the statement upon the Greekness of the Macedonians. The more usual *almost Greek in language* would have vitiated the effect.

In the following sentence, Wells alters the personal pronoun *he* to the proper noun *Philip* for the sake of clarity. To say that Philip turned "this little state into a great one" points to an admirable feat. However, before the book reached its final form, probably in galley proof, this sentence is altered to read, "Philip made this little *barbaric* state into a great one [my italics]," making Philip seem still more heroic and capable. The semicolon at the end of this clause unites it with the statement that follows; but in the original typescript, the statement breaks down when Wells calls Philip's military organization "official"; this word suggests formality and protocol and does not speak to effectiveness, a fact that Wells must have realized when he inserted *efficient* for *official. Got* in "he had got most of Greece into one confederacy" was not altered to *brought* until some time further along. The selection of *brought,* of course, ascribes to Philip much more responsibility for the organization of the confederacy than *got,* even in Wells' British usage, implied.

The deletion of "in nothing more plainly than" and its replacement with "not so much in these matters as" does little to alter meaning or tone. It merely replaces a less than graceful statement with one that is somewhat more graceful. The point made in this sentence—that Philip was training his son to succeed him—is driven home in the 1920 edition by the addition of the sentence, "He is one of the few monarchs in history who cared for his successor." He then expands "Aristotle was one of the several tutors his father chose for him" to "Aristotle was *but* one of the several *able* tutors his father chose for him [my italics]." The addition of *but* reinforces *several*; *able,* of course, identifies a quality in the tutor, again intensifying the force of what Wells seeks to convey.

The only other subsequent alterations of the typescript reproduced in Figure 1 occur in the last three lines: the correction of
misbehave for *behave* and the substitution of *had triumphed* for
the less active, somewhat anonymous *were triumphant.*

The pages reproduced here do not bear the extensive alterations
that the pages of some authors do; but they serve well to demonstrate how a writer, even so competent a writer as H. G. Wells,
goes about the task of improving an early draft. Some writers,
like Whitman with *Leaves of Grass,* continue to revise a single
work, expanding it, making significant deletions, and generally
reworking it for long periods, sometimes coming up with new
editions that are drastically different from earlier ones. Other
writers revise less and move on from the publication of one work
to the preparation of another. But it is safe to assume that nearly
all writers of stature have gained that stature because the revision
process has been a fundamental part of their process of composing.
Revision—or the reseeing—of any piece of writing is essential to
its success. Certainly anyone who would teach another to write
would be remiss in not teaching revision as a fundamental part
of the writing process.

Insights from the Blind:
Composing without Revising

Anne Ruggles Gere
University of Washington

In this discussion I describe the writing process of a blind writer who does virtually no revising. While it might seem that the behavior of a nonreviser has no place in a discussion of revising, the deprivation model, long popular in medical research, deduces function by examining the features that occur in its absence. Studies of individuals lacking an enzyme, for example, provide information about the enzyme's function; in this case, examining the behavior of a nonreviser increases understanding of revising. The deprivation model has a double function here because absence of sight contributes directly to the lack of revising. The word *revision* connotes re-seeing or taking a new view of what has been produced. Vision or seeing is at the heart of revising, and studying the work of a blind nonreviser enlarges our understanding of this part of the composing process.

At least two researchers have noted the role of sight in the rescanning which is part of revising. Robert Zoellner comments on behavior characteristic of many students during in-class writing: "While I have no hard data on scribal ritualism in college students, unobtrusive eye-movement counts during test periods make it clear that many students cannot write a sentence until they have re-read the previous sentence from three to ten times."[1] Although the compulsive activity Zoellner describes does not constitute actual revising, it emphasizes the role sight plays in revision. A more dramatic portrayal of the part sight has in revising appears in the discussion of James Britton and his colleagues on the irregular rate of writing production:

> We can see a writer scanning back over what has been done, and possibly making alterations; this, even if it takes up comparatively little of the pause-time, may be quite important. On one occasion, four members of this research team tried writing with worn-out ball-point pens. We couldn't,

> therefore, see what we had written, but we used carbon paper
> so that what we wrote could be read later. We were acutely
> uncomfortable. When we wrote letters to an absent member
> of the team about what we were doing, and when we reported
> recent experiences in a straightforward narrative, we were
> able to complete the task with only a few blunders; but when
> we tried to formulate theoretical principles, even on a topic
> very familiar to us all, and when we tried to write poems,
> we were defeated. We just could not hold the thread of an
> argument or the shape of a poem in our minds, because
> scanning back was impossible. As we expected, the carbon
> copies showed many inconsistencies and logical and syntac-
> tical discontinuities. They were, in fact, useless.[2]

These members of Britton's team found that inability to rescan
as they wrote made it impossible for them to write in some modes.
Zoellner's and Britton's observations and Janet Emig's exhorta-
tion that researchers give more attention to organic structures in
writing[3] led me to learn more about the role sight plays in revising.

To understand more about the nature of seeing, I turned to
philosophy. Philosophers, beginning with Aristotle and Plato,
have debated the relationship between seeing and knowing. In
Aristotle's terms, sensory experience provides data for mental
processes; what we see, touch, smell, hear, and taste interacts with
the imagination—the intermediary between sensory perception
and memory—to become mental processes. Thought depends upon
what the senses extract from the external world. In Plato's terms,
the external world has much less importance because sensory
experience merely approximates Platonic Ideas or images of
higher reality. These Ideas provide a model for the "darkling
organs of sense," and the mind's optimal function is to recall
the Ideas initiated by what the senses can perceive. Each age
from classical times to the present has emphasized either an
Aristotelian or a Platonic view of the senses; during the medieval
period, for example, thought was described in Aristotle's terms,
while the Renaissance adapted Plato's views. In later centuries
the debate took new form. During the seventeenth century William
Molyneux asked his friend John Locke whether a blind person
who gained sight would be able to identify a cube and a globe
from looking at them. Locke joined Molyneux in a negative reply,
arguing against the interrelationship of the senses. As Michael
Morgan explains: Locke couldn't agree to a "common representa-
tional system for the different senses, because such a scheme
implies an innate supra-sensible structure to the mind. An innate
supra-sensible scheme downgrades the role of observation through

the senses and, ultimately, strengthens the case for authoritarian philosophical systems at the expense of free inquiry."[4] Locke's insistence, despite its contradictions and ambiguities, on the autonomy of the senses opened the way for empirical methodology and the disciplines it spawned. Despite their recognition of Locke's contributions, few contemporary philosophers share his views on the autonomy of the senses. Nelson Goodman's description of the interrelationship of sight with other senses typifies the modern view:

> The eye comes always ancient to its work, obsessed by its own past and by old and new insinuations of the ear, nose, tongue, fingers, heart and brain. It functions not as an instrument self-powered and alone, but as a dutiful member of a complex and capricious organism. Not only how but what it sees is regulated by need and prejudice. It selects, rejects, organizes, discriminates, associates, classifies, analyzes, constructs. It does not so much mirror as take and make. . . .[5]

Psychologists corroborate this view of the interrelationship of the senses, and they point to the connections between sight and mental processes. Early language development, for example, depends upon vision in the stages where labeling objects plays a major role. Blind children develop language much more slowly than their sighted peers. Eve Clark suggests that earliest semantic features may be derived directly from sight through combinations of perceptual features. "Thus perceptual features themselves may well belong to the set of universal semantic primities."[6] While lack of sight inhibits their early language development, blind children catch up with their sighted peers when concepts such as past and future develop and language becomes less context-dependent.

Medical and psychological research provides further insight into the nature of vision. Because touch, the primary means by which blind children perceive the world, is linear, blind children usually conceptualize in linear fashion.[7] This difference in conceptualization may explain the differences in EEG patterns for blind and sighted adults and the differences in brain hemisphere activity in blind and sighted readers.[8] "Blindisms" or the stereotypical movements common to those who have never received visual feedback are often evident among the blind. However, blind people often make physical movements that are not blindisms.[9] These movements facilitate encoding for the blind just as simi-

lar movements aid sighted writers. Several researchers have as-
serted a relationship between muscle activity and organization of
thought and have suggested that body movement is an important
part of speech.[10] Because of their disability, blind people develop
compensatory skills. One of the most prominent of these is memory, and their prodigious memory feats have been chronicled by
a number of researchers.[11]

Armed with an appreciation for the complex relationship between sight and thought and with the suggestion that blind
people may employ slightly different cognitive procedures than
their sighted peers, I investigated the composing process of a
blind writer to learn more about revising.

Jackie, the subject of this study, suffered retrolental fibroplasia
from overexposure to incubator oxygen as an infant and has
never had any useful vision. Because there was no program for
blind children in the community where she was raised, Jackie
attended school with sighted children, receiving special help a
few hours a day and working with her parents at home. The
younger of two children, Jackie was encouraged to develop fully
her tactile senses. Her parents' willingness to allow her to experiment no doubt explains much of Jackie's independence of spirit.
Those who know her describe her as an original and critical
thinker. Now a woman in her early thirties, Jackie holds a B.A.
in English and an M.A. in educational psychology. In addition to
holding a Civil Service position, Jackie has traveled extensively
in the United States and abroad and has a variety of interests,
including horticulture and music.

Jackie's first reading and writing experiences were in braille,
but she learned to type during the first and second grade. Typing
allowed her to communicate in writing with the sighted world,
and she recalls it as an important breakthrough. From her earliest
years Jackie was interested in writing and did a good deal of
self-sponsored writing. Her first story, recounting a visit to a
bakery, was published when she was in the second grade. In
addition to writing stories, poems, and song lyrics and music,
Jackie wrote many letters. This pattern of self-sponsored writing
has continued for Jackie; she keeps a journal and writes prose
and poetry for herself.

Jackie's interest in writing distinguished her from the rest of
her family; however, the family has a rich tradition of oral expression. Jackie describes her grandmother's neighborhood gossip as
fascinating narrative, and she recalls many of her father's hunt-

ing tales. The existence of these storytellers adds an important dimension to the family's expressive history, especially for a blind child.

This study is divided into two parts: an examination of the composing process under experimental conditions and an exploration of school-sponsored writing through interview and examination of texts. Both parts use the case study method and share the limited generalizability of this method, although this limitation is countered by the thoroughness and detail the case study permits.

Composing under Experimental Conditions

Meetings between the subject and the interviewer were held on four afternoons at one-week intervals. These meetings were held at the subject's apartment, where typewriter and braillewriters were available, and the subject was encouraged to use the medium most appropriate for the writing task. Jackie was asked to produce two pieces of writing at each meeting, taking as long as she wished and using either typewriter or braillewriter. No length for either writing was specified. Both pieces of writing for each afternoon were written in response to the same task; first Jackie wrote as she normally would, then she composed aloud. This order was preserved at all four meetings. Instructions for successive tasks were these:

1. Tell the story of something that has happened to you; it could be frightening or pleasant, but recount the event as you might tell it to a friend.
2. Describe a procedure or skill you know well to a novice who wishes to learn the skill or procedure.
3. Outline two theoretical positions and then argue for one or the other as you would for a group of peers in your field.
4. Begin a short story or poem just as you would if you were writing one for yourself.

Jackie found the fourth task very difficult to accomplish in an experimental setting, and a discussion of two poets was substituted for the composing aloud portion of that day's task. The following are excerpts from Jackie's responses to these tasks.

Task 1: Narrative

I had always wanted to hitchhike. I finally did it when I was in the Peace Corps. I met a Canadian, Lynn, and we decided to go to Nicaragua. He wanted to get to a place on the Atlantic Coast called Bluefields, only accessible by jungle riverboat or airplane. It sounded exciting, and somewhat dangerous, to me—just the stuff for a great adventure! I took my guide dog, and we were off.

We rode a Volkswagen-type bus down the mountains, twisting and turning until we reached the Pan-American highway, then caught a big Greyhound-type bus from there across the border between Honduras and Nicaragua to just outside of Monagua. There, we slept out in Lynn's tent. (He was living out of his pack and traveling through Central America.) We heated some water on his tiny gas stove and had a light supper, and went to bed. We were in a field. The next day we caught a ride on the road leading toward the river that we would eventually go down to reach Bluefields. But the ride finished, and there were no other cars on that road, for it seemed like hours. Finally, we caught a dilapidated bus which went over very rough dirt roads till it reached the "hotel" right at the source of this river. (I can't remember what the river is called.) We ate a late dinner there, and tried to sleep. The hotel was a wood-frame building, very old; water was turned off at ten and we did not finish dinner until after ten. Toilets didn't flush, and we dipped water out of a tank. It was none too clean. The beds were straw, filled with God-knows-what. The night was hot and humid, full of mosquitos, and I felt dirty all over. . . .

Task 2: Description of Procedure (obedience training)

Many people say they want to train dogs but don't know how. They seem to think that dog-training is a mysterious art that only a few are privy to. However, dogs are very amenable to training, and the art is only that the master become amenable to doing it. It takes some time and work, and some gift for putting oneself in the place of the dog to try to guess what the dog will be able to understand, realizing that he does not understand words but only tone of voice.

To train a puppy to lie down is really simple. You bribe him. Not with food (although food could be used) but with tone of voice. Puppies love to please. They catch enthusiasm and pleasure from you in your tone of voice. Puppies also love to be petted and played with. They derive pleasure from your touch, from your petting them, scratching their ears and tummies. Hands are your communicators, as well as your voice.

First get your dog's attention. Have him come to you and stand in front of you. Remove all bones, balls and other toys that may be distracting. Give him the gentle but firm command, "Rover (or whatever his name is), down." Put your hand on the ground and at the same time, pat the ground with your hand. Put your hand palm up and wiggle the fingers. As the puppy noses your hand, gently push his back end down with your other hand, or move the "decoy" hand a little forward to encourage his nose and body to follow. When he is down at both ends, immediately pet and praise him, repeating the word "down" and telling him (or her) how clever he (she) is. . . .

Task 3: Theoretical Position (nature versus nurture)

Other than looking similar and therefore being confusing to those of us who by nature can't spell, nature and nurture are two opposite concepts held up in educational circles, like the red banner that bullfighters use, for educators to fight over. "Nature" is the idea that the child—that poor little collicky baby—has language already built in in his head somewhere, even though all he says is "Wah"—and somehow this language "program" will develop when it needs to, despite what is happening to him. The "nurture" idea in its pure form, says that Johny gets all the info from what happens to him as he grows up, that he gets his language by imitating those around him.

As usual in these "fights" I beg off. I can counter or support both arguments. If Johny says "wah" and never encounters anybody else saying anything else, he will always say "wah" and that will be all. So much for the nature argument. On the other hand, if Johny does have input other than "wah" he will imitate, but he will also develop language in a certain order, according to rules utilized by human infants around the world, and he will "discover" rules within whatever language (or languages) he is acquiring. . . .

Task 4: Short Story

The store aisle was empty for the moment. The boy looked around furtively, grabbed a handful of packages of gum and stuffed them in his pocket. He sauntered carelessly down the aisle, turned down another one. He found the box of Tide detergent his mother wanted and approached the check stand. The clerk rang up the soap, put the sales slip in the bag and he walked toward the door.

"Wait a second. What's that in your pocket?" a man dressed in the store uniform stood beside him.

"Nothing," the boy said, inching toward the door.

"Let's see," the man said.

"No, it's my stuff," the boy said. "I didn't take anything...."

Jackie was observed during the eight writing episodes, and the composing aloud was taped for later transcription. Elapsed time for writing, including pauses and length of pauses, was noted for each piece of writing. As soon as Jackie declared a piece of writing completed, we discussed the decisions she had made as she was composing.

Jackie's composing process omits stages identified by research with sighted writers. Research has delineated stages which include prewriting, planning, composing, stopping, reformulating, rereading, contemplating finished product, and handing in of product.[12] In all but one kind of writing Jackie did no rereading, and she never contemplated a finished product. She elected to type everything except task four, thus eliminating the possibility of scanning back or contemplating what she had written. When questioned about particular sentences in the writing, however, she recalled what she had said very clearly. Her memory compensated in large measure for her inability to see what she had said.

When typing, Jackie subvocalized much of her writing, yet she was unaware of this behavior, and it did not cease when I called her attention to it. Research indicates the value of private speech for problem-solving,[13] and Jackie's subvocalizing seemed to function in much the same way. In his study of the composing processes of seven-year-old children, Donald Graves notes a considerable amount of accompanying language (ranging from overt talk to whispering) and attributes it to the reactive writer who needs an immediate rehearsal in order to write.[14] Like Graves's reactive writer, Jackie seems to require an immediate rehearsal as she writes, and she rarely contemplates her written product. Surprisingly, despite her subvocalization, Jackie found it very difficult to compose aloud while writing and after several attempts evolved a system of repeating a sentence aloud after she had typed it. Although she was asked to compose aloud at each writing session, she never completed a full piece of writing in that mode. Typically she would repeat sentences aloud for the first fifty to seventy-five words and then, absorbed in the writing itself, return to her usual habit of subvocalizing as she typed. At no time did she engage in the kind of oral discourse reproduced in Emig's protocols, and only when she used the braillewriter did she offer reflections—comments on word choice, explanation of changes— on her writing.

Jackie evinced considerable facial expression as she composed. She held her head erect as she wrote, nodded and made other movements with her head, and often smiled or laughed about what she was composing. These movements were not "blindisms" but were varied and resembled the kinesthetic communications of sighted people. There are at least three explanations for these movements: (1) motor activity plays a central role in verbal encoding; (2) blind writers serve as an immediate audience for their own composing; (3) lacking visual feedback, blind writers persist in behaviors repressed by sighted writers. Jackie's similarity to Graves's reactive writer suggests that some of the behavior, particularly the smiling and laughing, functioned as audience reac-

Table 1

Summary of Variables in Composing Process

Writer's responses	Typewriter						Braillewriter	
	Narrative		Description of procedure		Theoretical position		Short story	
	Regular process	Composing aloud	Regular process	Composing aloud	Regular process	Composing aloud	Regular process	Composing aloud
Prewriting time	45"	65"	5"	15"	10"	30"	240"	10"
Composing time	12'	7'	14'	10'	10'	13'	12'	8'
Total words written	489	244	450	330	243	349	112	194
Composing rate (words per minute)	40.7	34.8	32	33	24.3	26.8	9.3	16.1
Total number of pauses	6	9	4	4	5	10	6	18
Mean length of pauses	5.6"	11.2"	6.7"	7.2"	8"	12.2"	12"	13.3"

tion and supports the hypothesis that the composing process of blind writers is a highly externalized one in which audience takes a dominant role from the earliest stages of composing.

Fluency in writing distinguishes Jackie from sighted writers examined in other studies. Sharon Pianko reports composing rates of 9.31 and 9.29 words per minute for remedial and traditional college freshmen respectively.[15] As Table 1 indicates, Jackie's rate of composing varied with the writing task, but her mean composing rate (Table 2) was 31.9 words per minute when she composed at the typewriter. Part of this remarkable fluency can be explained by Jackie's infrequent and relatively short pauses. While Pianko reports means of 11.40 and 23.43 pauses for remedial and traditional students respectively, Jackie's average number of pauses while typing was 6.2. As Table 2 indicates, both these patterns changed dramatically when Jackie switched to the braillewriter. Her composing rate dropped to an average of 12.7 words per minute, still higher than the writing rate of Pianko's subjects, but considerably lower than any of Jackie's typing rates. Similarly, Jackie's average number of pauses nearly doubled when she used the braillewriter. Her mean of 12.0 pauses falls between that of the two groups in Pianko's study. This increase in number of pauses correlates directly with Jackie's scanning back; roughly half her pauses with the braillewriter included rereading the preceding words on a line—although occasionally she reread an entire paragraph. Jackie's typing fluency applies to most of her school-sponsored writing as well. Although this study cannot provide precise composing rates for papers produced earlier, her rate seems to be well above fifteen words per minute for a footnoted research paper.

Table 2

Means for Two Writing Media

Writer's responses	Typewriter	Braillewriter
Prewriting time	28″	120″
Composing time	11′	10′
Total words written	350	153
Composing rate (words per minute)	31.9	12.7
Total number of pauses	6.2	12
Total length of pauses	8.5″	12.6″

As Table 2 shows, Jackie's mean prewriting time for typewritten prose was 28 seconds, considerably less than the mean of 86 seconds for college freshmen reported by Pianko. Planning and prewriting occurred simultaneously as Jackie decided upon a topic, considered the ideas she wanted to include, and selected a general direction for her writing. Although she claimed that she didn't know exactly what she would say until she actually wrote it, the infrequency and brevity of her pauses allowed her little time for planning during the actual writing. When she composed at the typewriter, Jackie never revised—and she wrote only one draft. Her typewritten manuscripts were mechanically perfect; she corrected occasional typos as they occurred, and she observed conventions scrupulously. Once, in eight writing episodes, Jackie hesitated and asked for help in thinking of a word. Although she had access to both braillewriter and typewriter and was encouraged to use either for any of the writing tasks, Jackie elected the typewriter for all but one writing task. She explained that she preferred to use the typewriter for most things because words flow more easily when she types.

Ease of production, however, is not always the determining factor for Jackie's decision about means for writing. In addition to the typewriter, which she uses for most school-sponsored writing, she has two braillewriters, a Perkins and a Stainsby. The Perkins, a typical American type, is a table model resembling a typewriter. By pushing the six keys Jackie can produce face-up braille available for scanning, much as typewritten words are available to a sighted writer. As noted earlier, Jackie elected the braillewriter for writing her short story, and using the Perkins model she did a good deal of rescanning as she composed.

Unlike the Perkins, the Stainsby brailler, a lap-sized machine that can be held closer to the writer, produces reverse image braille that cannot be read until the page is removed from the machine. Jackie uses the Stainsby for writing in her journal, maintaining that physical proximity to the brailler is important when she is writing about emotionally charged topics. This proximity apparently outweighs the drawback of the reversed image. Although Jackie's journal was not included in this investigation, she claims that she writes as fluently there as at the typewriter because the emotional energy behind her writing generates a flow similar to what she usually experiences at the typewriter.

During interviews after she had completed a composing task, Jackie often commented that she knew what the first paragraph would say as she typed the title of her paper. She also observed that she rarely thinks of individual words as she writes, concentrating instead on images and the larger context of what she is saying. Preliminary investigation of brain activity during verbal tasks indicates that the right hemisphere is active when blind adults read while the left hemisphere takes a dominant role in the reading of sighted adults.[16] This right hemisphere activity during verbal tasks and evidence that EEG's of the blind differ substantially from those of the sighted clarify and lend support to Jackie's claim of writing from images rather than words.

School-sponsored Writing

Despite the fact that Jackie had been an excellent student throughout her school years, her school-sponsored writing has meant little to her. She can recall few of her writing assignments. In fact, she believes that her decision to major in English as an undergraduate probably hindered her writing. Her literature courses emphasized the aesthetic quality of masterpieces, making her feel inadequate to try writing because she could not match the standards of what she was reading.

One school-sponsored writing task, however, did make a considerable impression and contributed, Jackie claims, to her ability as a writer. A braille teacher, herself blind, insisted that Jackie make braille copies of her reading assignments. This process of copying during the early grades gave Jackie direct experience with the conventions of written language. Punctuation, paragraphing, and sentence structure became very clear to Jackie through these copying exercises, and she feels that this copying practice freed her from thinking about surface details and allowed her to concentrate on what she wanted to say.

Jackie offered two recent papers for analysis; both had been written for educational psychology courses she took to complete her M.A. degree. The assignment for each was similar: Write a research paper to be turned in at the end of the term. Both were what Jackie calls her "first-draft/last-draft" papers, finished products produced in one sitting. One, a discussion of Samuel Gridley Howe's role in American education, began with typical research work. Jackie read several books on Howe and made braille notes for later reference. Shortly before the paper was due she had a period of procrastination when she thought about her topic, read her notes, worried over the paper, but didn't do anything about it. Then, the night before the paper was due, she typed steadily for five hours to produce a twelve-page manuscript. For this paper, as for most of her writing, Jackie worked on large units without a break. She stopped between units to think about where the next section would go, but she made little reference to her notes. As she put it, "By the time I began to write the paper I felt I knew Howe well enough to predict what he would say in a given situation." A reader helped Jackie check for typing errors, but with minor corrections the manuscript Jackie composed in one sitting was the "A" paper she turned in.

The first-draft/last-draft process is a typical one for Jackie's school-sponsored writing. When compared with other descriptions of the composing process, Jackie's prewriting and planning stages are extraordinarily long while her reformulating and contemplating of product are virtually nonexistent. Memory plays a much larger role in her writing than it does for sighted writers because she is drawing her material from memory at the same time that she is remembering the structure of her plan for the paper and keeping track of the words she last wrote.

Earlier in her school career Jackie often used a more complicated process for writing papers. She would write the paper in braille where she could "see" it, revise in braille, and then type a final draft. Jackie abandoned this procedure because it was too time-consuming and didn't seem to produce any better results than the first-draft/last-draft method. It was school-sponsored writing in a journalism class that freed Jackie to compose at the typewriter. Journalism taught her to get a whole story in her head and to type it at one sitting, and she was able to transfer this ability to other writing tasks. She learned how to make her writing move continually forward.

Although the two school-sponsored papers were on different topics—Howe's role in American education and "The Blind Infant's Discovery of Dimension, Distance and Object Concepts"— both have an essentially narrative structure. The first places Howe in history and follows the events of his life, tracing their influence on American education. The paper on blind infants, although based on research and carefully annotated, also employs chronological structure, following the infant's development from birth through the first year of life. Similarly, the eight papers written under experimental conditions followed a narrative pattern. Sheila Fraiberg, we are reminded, found that because the sense of touch requires linear approaches to physical objects, blind children conceptualize in linear fashion.[17] While Jackie's case does not include enough writing samples to support definitive conclusions, it suggests the importance of examining further the characteristic methods of organization used by blind writers. It may be that the linear conceptualizations Fraiberg found in blind infants also shape the thinking of blind adults.

Implications

Jackie's case has implications for teachers and researchers interested in revising. Teachers frequently lament the lack of detail and specificity in student writing and urge young writers to "show not tell." To show something requires the ability to "see" it, an ability not limited to the sighted as Jackie's writing samples indicate. However, this study and Pianko's observation about less able writers whose eyes distract rather than provide insight into their work suggest that the ability to "see" is not inherent in all students but must be acquired. George Hillocks has demonstrated the efficacy of procedures for increasing student powers of observation: students trained to use their eyes more effectively produce revisions with greater specificity and detail than those who have not learned to use their eyes carefully.[18] Similarly, the revision strategies recommended by Lee Odell and Joanne Cohick emphasize helping students to develop their "vision" through taking a variety of perspectives.[19] These and similar methods should be used in the classroom to help students develop the ability to "see" and therefore revise.

Another implication for teachers concerns the relationship between revising and modes of writing. Whether one uses James Britton's terms—expressive, transactional, and poetic—or James Moffett's—egocentric and decentered writing—or Linda Flower's —writer-based and reader-based prose—contemporary theorists seem to agree that revising from one mode to another involves psychological as well as formal dimensions. The fact that all of Jackie's writing examined in this study was essentially narrative and the fact that all of this writing had not been revised raises questions about the advisability of teaching, say, exposition in isolation from narrative. Revising may be the link between modes of writing, and teachers should exploit this link by asking students to revise the same piece of writing in several ways.

Audience becomes a major factor when writers revise, and Jackie's self-proclaimed ability to visualize her audience may explain, in part, how it is possible for her to write without revising. Teachers who designate an audience in writing assignments can help students develop the ability to visualize audiences for themselves. Teachers might also consider fostering tutorial dialogue

in their classes. Because of her handicap Jackie spent part of
each school day, especially in the early grades, in a special class
where she received considerable individual attention. This opportunity for conversation with a tutoring adult, she claims, helped
her learn to visualize audiences for her writing. Joan Tough's
study of language development suggests that dialogue with adults
contributes to successful communication for sighted as well as
blind students; such dialogue enables students to develop a sense
of perspective: "If language is to provide a means of exchanging
meanings, then those who communicate must project into the
meanings of each other. Thus taking part in dialogue necessarily
demands a projection into the perspective of the other, alternating
with an inward reflection on the meanings that are to be offered
to the other."[20] By fostering tutorial dialogue in their classes,
teachers may be able to help students develop a sense of audience
that will enable them to revise effectively.

Jackie's remarkable fluency suggests another implication for
teachers. While simple production of a great many words per
minute should not be a goal for any writer, Peter Elbow, among
others, has argued that fluency aids early stages of writing.[21]
The methods he proposes deliberately eliminate pauses in writing and encourage writers to separate drafting from revising.
All writing, like all reading, should not proceed at the same
rate, and nonstop writing such as Elbow advocates may help
students to vary their rate according to the task, thus enabling
students to separate their drafting from their revising. Fluency,
of course, varies with the medium for writing. A few teachers,
Mina Shaughnessy among them, have noted that composing at
the typewriter aids student writers,[22] but few classroom settings
allow students to find the medium with which they feel most
comfortable. By encouraging students to experiment with various
means for writing, teachers may be able to help them find one
that enhances their revising.

Jackie's insistence upon the importance of her early copying
exercises suggests that teachers reconsider outmoded pedagogy
that places emphasis on dictation, memorizing, and copying.
While none of these methods has intrinsic value, the combination
may help students develop internal standards necessary for revising. As Richard Beach has noted, many students cannot judge
strengths and weaknesses of their own writing: "The fact that
students often do not revise their drafts reflects their inability to
effectively evaluate their own writing."[23] By helping students to
internalize models of excellence in writing, teachers may help

them to improve their ability to evaluate and thus to revise their writing.

In addition to these implications for teachers—that they offer instruction in "seeing," that they encourage revision into various modes, that they foster tutorial dialogue, that they encourage students to develop fluency as writers, and that they help students internalize good models—Jackie's case has implications for researchers interested in revision. In his study of children's writing, Donald Graves describes reactive and reflective writers:

> Children who were identified as reactive showed erratic problem solving strategies, the use of overt language to accompany prewriting and composing phases, isolation that evolved in action-reaction couplets, proofreading at the word unit level, a need for immediate rehearsal in order to write, rare contemplation or reviewing of products, characterizations that exhibited general behaviors similar to their own, a lack of a sense of audience when writing, and an inability to use reasons beyond the affective domain in evaluating their writing.

> Children who were identified as reflective showed little rehearsal before writing, little overt language to accompany writing, periodic rereadings to adjust small units of writing at the word or phrase level, growing sense of audience connect[ed] with their writing, characterizations that exhibit general behaviors similar to their own in the expression of feelings, and the ability to give examples to support their reasons for evaluating writing.[24]

While these two terms provide researchers a means for categorizing the behaviors of some writers, Jackie's behavior suggests that the terms should not be accepted as typologies without further investigation. Jackie shared the reactive writer's use of overt language, need for immediate rehearsal, and rare contemplation of product; however, she resembled the reflective writer in her sense of audience and in her ability to give reasons for her evaluation of her own writing. Although Jackie may not be a typical writer, her behavior calls the integrity of these categories into question and points to the need for further research into behaviors that identify types of writers and revisers.

A related question of categories also has implications for researchers. Jackie's ability to write demonstrates the interaction of the senses because she uses touch, smell, taste, and hearing to compensate for the sight she lacks. Learning theory proposes that some individuals rely primarily on sight, others on sound, and still others on kinesthetics as their primary means of assimilating information. Jackie's reliance on senses other than sight suggests that the same variation in dominant channel may well exist for writers as well as learners. Malcolm Cowley reflects on the senses and composing: "I have often heard it said by psychiatrists that writers belong to the 'oral type.' The truth seems to be that most of them are manual types. Words are not merely sounds for them, but magical designs that their hands make on paper."[25] This statement, like the case study of Jackie, may represent an idiosyncratic viewpoint, but even with its limited applicability, it points to the need for research into the dominant mode of writers.

The most encompassing research question has its roots in the ancient debate about the relationship of senses to thought. Many composition theorists, drawing on insights from cognitive psychology, postulate cognitive processes underlying the composing process, pointing to features in discourse or aspects of invention that illustrate these processes.[26] Research should, of course, pursue the directions suggested by these theorists, but such research will be enhanced by more explicit attention to the role of the senses in writing and revising.

A final research question suggested by Jackie's case concerns the relationship between writing and memory. Generations of thinkers have argued that writing decreases memory,[27] and recent research indicates that people from nonliterate cultures have much greater powers of memory than those from cultures with a high degree of literacy.[28] Yet, Jackie's remarkable memory indicates that writing need not diminish memory's powers, and her ability to hold content information, general structure of her writing, and immediately preceding word in her mind simultaneously demonstrates how a well-developed memory can aid writing. Researchers, using memory protocols, training exercises, and a variety of other methods, might well investigate the relationship between memory and revising.

Although this study raises more questions than it answers and ranges beyond revision to other aspects of the composing process, it affirms the essential relationship between "vision" and revision, and it underlines the importance of revising in the composing process.

Notes

1. Robert Zoellner, "Talk-Write: A Behavioral Pedagogy for Composition," *College English* 30 (1969): 271.

2. James Britton, Tony Burgess, Nancy Martin, Alex McLeod, and Harold Rosen, *The Development of Writing Abilities (11-18)*, Schools Council Research Studies (London: Macmillan Education, 1975), p. 35.

3. Janet Emig, "Hand, Eye, Brain: Some 'Basics' in the Writing Process," in *Research on Composing: Points of Departure*, eds. Charles R. Cooper and Lee Odell (Urbana, Ill.: National Council of Teachers of English, 1978), p. 59.

4. Michael Morgan, *Molyneux's Question* (New York: Cambridge University Press, 1977), p. 14.

5. Nelson Goodman, *Languages of Art* (Indianapolis: Hackett, 1976), pp. 7-8.

6. Eve Clark, "What's in a Word? On the Child's Acquisition of Semantics in His First Language," in *Cognitive Development and the Acquisition of Language*, ed. Timothy Moore (New York: Academic Press, 1973), p. 104.

7. Shelia Fraiberg, *Insights from the Blind: Comparative Studies of Blind and Sighted Infants* (New York: Basic Books, 1977), pp. 32-35.

8. J. Jacquay, A. Piraux, and G. Noel, "Hemispheric Patterns at Rest and While Reading in the Normal Adult, the Normal Child and the Blind: A Quantitative Rheoencephalographic Investigation," *ACTA Neurologica Scandinavica* 56 (1977): 528-29.

9. R. Blass, N. Freedman, and I. Steingart, "Body Movement and Verbal Encoding in the Congenitally Blind," *Perceptual and Motor Skills* 39 (1974): 290-92.

10. See Jean Piaget, *The Psychology of Intelligence* (Totowa, N.J.: Littlefield, Adams, 1960); or A. R. Luria, *The Nature of Human Conflicts* (New York: Liveright, 1932).

11. For a summary of this work see J. Juurma, *Ability Structure and Loss of Vision* (New York: American Foundation for the Blind, 1967).

12. See Janet Emig, *The Composing Processes of Twelfth Graders* (Urbana, Ill.: National Council of Teachers of English, 1971); Terry A. Mischel, "A Case Study of a Twelfth-grade Writer," *Research in the Teaching of English* 8 (1974): 303-14; and Sharon Pianko, "A Description of the Composing Processes of College Freshman Writers," *Research in the Teaching of English* 13 (1979): 5-22.

13. B. Bloom and L. Broder, "Problem Solving Processes of College Students," in *The Learning Process*, eds. T. Harris and W. Schamm (New York: Oxford University Press, 1961), pp. 59-79.

14. Donald H. Graves, "An Examination of the Writing Processes of Seven-Year-Old Children," *Research in the Teaching of English* 9 (1975): 230-32.

15. Sharon Pianko, "A Description of the Composing Processes of College Freshman Writers," *Research in the Teaching of English* 13 (1979): 13.

16. Jacquay et al., "Hemispheric Patterns," p. 529.

17. Fraiberg, *Insights from the Blind*, pp. 32-35.

18. See George Hillocks, Jr., *Observing and Writing*, Theory and Research into Practice (Urbana, Ill.: National Council of Teachers of

English, 1975); and George Hillocks, Jr., "The Effects of Observational Activities on Student Writing," *Research in the Teaching of English* 13 (1979): 23-35.

19. See Lee Odell and Joanne Cohick, "You Mean, Write It Over in Ink?" *English Journal* 64 (December 1975): 48-53.

20. Joan Tough, *The Development of Meaning* (New York: John Wiley, 1977), p. 175.

21. Peter Elbow, *Writing without Teachers* (New York: Oxford University Press, 1973), pp. 25-30.

22. See Mina P. Shaughnessy, *Errors and Expectations: A Guide for the Teacher of Basic Writing* (New York: Oxford University Press, 1977), p. 16; and Robbins Burling, "An Anthropologist among the English Teachers," *College Composition and Communication* 25 (1974): 234-42.

23. Richard Beach, "Self-Evaluation Strategies of Extensive Revisers and Nonrevisers," *College Composition and Communication* 27 (1976): 160.

24. Graves, "An Examination of the Writing Processes," p. 236.

25. Malcolm Cowley, ed., *Writers at Work: The "Paris Review" Interviews* (New York: Penguin, 1977), p. 16.

26. See Frank D'Angelo, *A Conceptual Theory of Rhetoric* (Cambridge, Mass.: Winthrop, 1975); Lee Odell, "Measuring Changes in Intellectual Processes as One Dimension of Growth in Writing," in *Evaluating Writing: Describing, Measuring, Judging,* eds. Charles Cooper and Lee Odell (Urbana, Ill.: National Council of Teachers of English, 1977); and Linda S. Flower and John R. Hayes, "Problem-Solving Strategies and the Writing Process," *College English* 39 (1977): 449-61.

27. See H. L. Bergson, *Matter and Memory* (New York: Macmillan Co., 1911); Plato, *Phaedrus,* trans. R. Heok (Cambridge, At the University Press, 1952); J. Rousseau, *Discourse upon the Origin and Foundation of the Inequality between Mankind* (London: R. & J. Dodsley, 1761).

28. See Alfred Lord, *The Singer of Tales* (Cambridge, Mass.: Harvard University Press, 1960); or S. Phillips, "Literacy as a Mode of Communication on the Warm Spring Indian Reservation," in *Foundations of Language Development,* ed. Eric Lenneberg (San Francisco: Academic Press, 1975), pp. 167-82.

The Pragmatics of Self-assessing

Richard Beach
University of Minnesota

Probably because students have a limited conception of revising as editing, they are often reluctant to assess their own writing ability with any degree of rigor or responsibility. My own research on taped self-assessments made by college students of their rough drafts found that students fell into two groups: extensive revisers and nonrevisers. Nonrevisers conceived of revising as polishing or editing drafts, while extensive revisers conceived of revising in terms of substantive changes in organization, logic, or support.[1]

Nonrevisers often limited their assessments to editing matters because, in the context of school writing, they were concentrating primarily on matters of form. They assumed that their instructor would respond to editorial correctness. In contrast, extensive revisers made more reference to a reader's response to their goals, beliefs, knowledge, or ideas. They had a different conception of teacher as audience, assuming that their instructor was responding to their pragmatic attempts to convince, request, alert. They were also more likely to infer intended effects on an audience and to compare these intended effects with what they assumed would be their actual effects. By sensing a disparity between intended and actual effects, they recognized the need for substantive revision.

One problem was soon clear: in order to predict responses, students had to create assumed audiences. Students in both groups had difficulty at the crucial point of inferring audience, a complex process that has intrigued rhetoricians for years. Even the inferences of extensive revisers about audience were often too general; they failed to define purpose and audience in terms of specific knowledge, beliefs, status. As a result, when they began to assess whether their writing had fulfilled their intentions, their judgments were too global; they didn't have specific enough criteria to make specific judgments. Had they defined audience in more specific terms, they would then have been able to assume the role of reader, adopting the perspective of a particular belief, knowledge framework, status, or purpose for reading.

Beginning with the prewriting stage, writers make inferences about their audience. In order to make these inferences, they use their assumptions about what their audience typically knows or believes about a topic as well as their assumptions about that audience's status, purpose for reading, and reading ability. These inferences are, of course, mere assumptions because writers usually don't actually know their audience. Even if they do, they often don't know what that audience may know or believe about a particular topic. If, at the prewriting stage, they assume that their audience knows little about a topic, they develop more information. If writers assume that their audience doesn't share their ideas, they tend to bolster their defense of these ideas. The ability to infer audience characteristics depends on a writer's prior social experience. A writer who is quite familiar with what state legislators typically know or believe about church/state relationships will, in planning a letter to a legislator on that issue, have less difficulty making assumptions about that legislator's characteristics than someone who knows little about legislators.

Let me illustrate how writers use these learned assumptions to make inferences about audience characteristics. A high school student is writing a memo to her male principal about her math teacher. When this student asked for help with a calculus problem, the teacher remarked that "girls often have trouble with math." The student has decided to complain to the principal that the remark was sexist. She hopes that the principal will do something about the teacher's behavior.

In making inferences about an audience's knowledge, a writer tries to determine what that audience knows about the topic as well as what that audience knows about the writer's knowledge. Our student doesn't know the principal very well. She knows that the math teacher frequently makes what she deems sexist remarks and gives more positive comments to males than to females. She doesn't know whether the principal knows that. She also knows that while the principal probably knows that such remarks constitute a violation of Title IX guidelines, the teacher may not. She also knows that she is a good math student because she has done well in three previous years of math and has no problems using math in her after-school job. Based on her intended effect, she attempts to sort out which of this information is most relevant.

Writers also infer audience characteristics by making assumptions about a group's beliefs or attitudes in regard to a particular topic or issue. If they assume an audience represents certain social, economic, religious, or cultural types, they can make further assumptions about its beliefs. Consider, for example, the young man who is writing a pamphlet about crime for distribution to a largely rural, elderly population. He assumes that because those readers reside in small towns, they may believe that crime occurs primarily in urban rather than in rural areas. They may also believe that there is less crime in small towns because "criminal types" don't reside there. By inferring these beliefs, he then knows that he will need to address these assumptions.

While our student knows that the principal knows about Title IX, she knows that she cannot necessarily assume that he also advocates following those guidelines. (These are healthy doubts; too often students are oblivious to the fact that their audience may have a different set of beliefs from their own; they simply assume that their audience shares their beliefs.) Our student also believes that the principal is fair-minded and open to reason in discipline cases or cases involving student/teacher conflict. She therefore decides that in order to appeal to the principal's fairness she needs to build carefully a case that the teacher's remark is sexist and detrimental to her performance in the class.

In making inferences about her own and the principal's beliefs and knowledge, the student also considers her own and the principal's status, authority, and rights. While these characteristics differ, for the sake of discussion I will lump them together under the category, *status*. Writers need to infer status in order to assess whether they have the ability or legitimacy to perform certain speech acts successfully. If, for example, they make a request but their audience knows that they lack the authority to make that request, the request will fail. If, however, writers know that they have the authority to make a request, they assume that their request will succeed. Writers further need to distinguish between status as constituted and projected by the acts within the text and their official public status, particularly if they know that their readers don't know their public status. This may be difficult for some writers, who egocentrically assume that their readers already know them, failing to recognize that they need to establish their status through their writing. Our student knows that the principal knows that she is active in student government. She is not sure how much weight that carries with the principal; however, as an up-and-coming student leader, she assumes that it is typically the case that the principal will have to work with her; to some degree, then, she believes that he needs to be accountable to her concerns.

Because our student knows that her own status is not as high as that of the principal, she assumes, based on her understanding of power relationships, that requesting, demanding, or ordering the principal to do something about the math teacher's remark won't work. She therefore decides to ask whether the teacher's act constitutes a violation of Title IX guidelines. She assumes that a student has the right to make such a request, and she hopes that the principal may correctly interpret her request for information as a request for action.

Writers infer an audience's purpose for reading in order to predict the expectations or conceptual schemes an audience brings to the text. Knowing that an audience is reading a text in order to know how to do something helps a writer define the information that audience is expecting—what it needs to know in order to perform a task successfully. Based on assumptions about the principal's job, our student infers that his purpose for reading her memo will be to find out what happened in the incident in order to decide what action to take.

Writers also need to consider the reading skills of their audience in order to make decisions about the readability (vocabulary, syntax, transitions) and logical structure of what they are writing. While it could be argued that the audience's reading ability is not a pragmatic concern of the writer, if readers experience comprehension difficulties, they may judge a writer's status, information, or skills negatively. If, for example, a writer fails to realize that his or her readers are not familiar with certain technical terms, the readers may infer that the writer was insensitive to their needs. Our student assumes that the principal's reading ability is relatively advanced and that, in order to impress him, she can use relatively formal vocabulary and syntax.

Now that our student has inferred audience characteristics, she is ready to draft her memo. She can shift her critical perspective to that of the principal, reading and responding to the draft from his perspective as she writes and revises.

When writers begin to assess their drafts from their audience's perspective, they can judge whether or not their drafts are appropriate or effective. Students are often given general criteria or rules to use in judging their writing because teachers and textbook writers assume that these rules are appropriate for all "good writing." These rules, however, do not allow for variation in intention, audience, or type of discourse. For example, the maxim "be specific," based on the general assumption that good writing is specific, may not be consistent with an author's intention—deliberately to avoid references to specific instances. Many of these textbook maxims, as E. D. Hirsch has demonstrated,[2] concern matters of readability: "use the active voice," "put the subject and verb near each other," etc. It is odd that texts do not draw on social conventions concerning appropriate or inappropriate behavior within a given context.

When writers know that an audience disagrees with their opinions, they know that they won't make much headway by rudely dismissing the opposition. Rather, they learn to operate according to certain pragmatic principles, one of which is to acknowledge an opposing opinion and then to refute it with counter evidence. When drafts deviate from these principles, writers may then judge the writing as inappropriate and revise accordingly. The principles have, therefore, served not only as tacit criteria for judging the writing but also as guidelines for defining the direction of revision. Writers continue to revise until they reach what they deem is the most appropriate option, given the inferences they have made about audience characteristics and the principles they have for assessing appropriateness. H. Paul Grice has identified four categories under which fall certain more specific maxims that govern the verbal exchange of information; these can also be used to judge the effectiveness or appropriateness of writing.[3]

1. Quantity: A speaker should be as informative as is required for the current purposes of the exchange and not more informative than is required. (Writers may use this maxim to judge the economy of their writing. Is the information presented essential or superfluous?)

2. Quality: A speaker should say only that which he or she believes to be true and for which there is adequate evidence. (Writers need to assess the nature and amount of the evidence they use to support their contentions, evidence that they believe is valid. They must also assess the truth of their claims against an audience's knowledge. If they know that their audience believes that X is false, they may not want to claim that X is true.)

3. Relation: A speaker should make his or her contribution relevant. (The relevance of various parts of writing depends on

the writer's own sense of purpose and upon how he or she
assesses the audience's knowledge, its needs, and its purpose
for reading.)

4. Manner: A speaker should be perspicuous and orderly, avoiding obscure expressions, ambiguity, and prolixity. (Writers,
as I have noted, need to evaluate the clarity of their writing
relative to the reading ability they assume their audience
has, eliminating, for example, technical terms their audience
wouldn't understand.)

To implement each of these maxims, writers rely on inferences
about audience characteristics, and this reliance is consistent
with Grice's conception of communication as governed by a con-
tractual agreement between speaker/writer and audience. Writers
can also use these maxims to formulate revisions when they
recognize that the effect of what they have written is at odds with
what they intended the writing to communicate. In order to reduce the dissonance, they search for options, testing each against
the appropriate principle. Recognizing, for example, that an audience hasn't been given enough information to perform the stipu-
lated task, writers add information until they know that the
audience has enough. Similarly, they can also determine when
they have given too much information.

The maxims also help writers judge whether they are overly
direct or blunt in their requests or in statements that the audience
may not want to hear. If writers believe that their writing is too
direct and thus violates the principle of politeness or diplomacy,
they may choose what William Labov and David Fanshell define
as a more mitigating form.[4] For example, a writer may begin with
a direct order or command ("You will find those books for me."),
which might then be revised to a more mitigating form ("You will
find those books for me, won't you?") or to an even more mitigating form ("Will you please find those books for me?"). Labov and
Fanshell note that references to the audience's needs or abilities
are often mitigating while references to their rights and obliga-
tions are aggravating. Of course, writers may also decide after
considering their options deliberately to choose not to be polite, to
"talk tough," and they will consequently use more direct forms.

Writers continue testing options until they discover which best
fulfills their intentions. Each option implies a different potential
effect, and so the writer thinks, "If I choose option A, my audience
may respond in manner B; if I choose C, they will respond in
manner D." Having inferred audience characteristics and having

relied on Grice's maxims, writers finally settle on one option as most effective or appropriate.

Let me illustrate how I might use these pragmatic considerations to judge and revise a piece of writing. For many cold Minnesota winters, I've been running during late afternoons in the University of Minnesota fieldhouse. A large sign spelled out the schedule: jogging 4:30 to 6:00. The track team always practiced until 4:30 and then cleared out to make way for duffers like me. So this year I went over one subzero afternoon at 4:30 only to discover that the schedule had been changed: joggers were not allowed to run until 6:00, presumably to allow the track team more time to practice.

I am irked, so I decide to write a memo to the recreational coordinator, who is in charge of "self-service" sports. My first inclination is simply to ask that the schedule be changed back to the original 4:30. Then, in thinking about my own and my audience's status, I realize that a direct request for action would probably fail. I have no power to make such a request, and the coordinator—one person within a complex bureaucracy of coaches and administrators—wouldn't be able to carry out the request. Right at the starting point, I begin to revise. As did the student writing the memo to her principal, I opt for a request for information because at least I want to determine some rationale for the change.

I suspect that the track coach wants more time for the team to practice and, given the status of intercollegiate sports at a Big Ten school, has prevailed over those responsible for "self-service" sports. Because the coordinator may not be pleased about the change, he may be willing to reveal information in order to shift the blame to the track coach. On the other hand, the coordinator may have made the decision, in which case he might interpret my request as challenging his competence.

I also believe that the coordinator believes that I don't know how the decision was made and that, as a member of the staff, I have a right to ask for the information. While the coordinator may not want to disclose too much, he could give me some information. As Labov and Fanshell note in defining conditions constituting requests for information, a speaker's right to make a request for information is general and constant. The coordinator may also believe that I would believe that he had something to hide if he did not respond to my request. I then start jotting down some notes, assessing each as I move toward a draft: "During the past six winters, I have enjoyed running in the fieldhouse during the late afternoons. As a former cross-country runner (I ran on the same team as Amby Burfoot and William Rogers), I look forward to running at the end of the day."

Here I am trying to establish my own status as a runner in an attempt to garner some sympathy from the coordinator, who I assume identifies with my interest in running. I then realize that the coordinator may not really want to know about my former running experience or teammates because that information isn't relevant or essential to his purpose for reading the memo; I would be in violation of Grice's maxim of relation. I also realize that I should mention that I am a faculty member in order to establish professional identification with a fellow staff member, an identification that should give my request for information greater legitimacy.

So I revise: "As a member of the faculty for the past six years, I have enjoyed using the fieldhouse during the late afternoons." And I go on to add more background: "In the past, runners could use the fieldhouse after 4:30, but now I discover that the track is not available for use until 6:00. I was surprised at this schedule change because the fieldhouse was always used quite heavily from 4:30 to 6:00."

In thinking over this section, I infer that the coordinator probably already knows that the fieldhouse was heavily used after 4:30, so that information may not be necessary. On the other hand, I decide to include the information because it does imply that I am not the only one who is affected by the schedule change, legitimatizing my right to request the information. So, in order to imply that I know that he knows all this, I insert "as you know," resulting in "because, as you know, the fieldhouse was always used quite heavily from 4:30 to 6:00."

I then turn to what I suspect is a key issue, the track team: "I don't know why the track team needs to monopolize the track all afternoon until 6:00." I decide this is a little strong; if my goal is to find out why and how the decision was made, I should not suggest that I already have an answer. I'm also making a claim I can't substantiate, a violation of Grice's quality maxim. Instead, I decide to drop my charge and explore the rationale for the schedule change: "In making this schedule change, were the persons who use the fieldhouse during this time ever consulted?"

While this request is consistent with what I want to know, the coordinator may interpret it as implying that users were not consulted, a reference to the users' rights, which could be aggravating rather than mitigating. Because I assume that the coordinator may not have been the only person making the decision and may, in fact, have argued against the change only to be overruled, I decide to imply that he may side with the users: "As recreational coordinator, I am sure that you wish to accommodate as many persons as possible at the most convenient time." Having implied that I believe that the coordinator is more accommodating than others (the track coach), I can then explicitly refer to these two groups: "When the decision was made, did the coaching and/or recreational staff consider the interests of busy faculty and staff members who can only use the track during this time?" I then realize that I am suggesting that the faculty holds equal power with the athletic staff, an implication that the coordinator may regard as a presumptuous power play. I delete "busy faculty and staff," which results in this statement: "When the decision was made, did the coaching and/or recreational staff consider the heavy use of the track during that time period?"

Then, to move to make my request: "Please tell me why this change was made." I sense that this is too direct, so I choose a more mitigating form: "I would be grateful if you would tell me why this change was made."

In all of this self-assessing, I can make inferences about hierarchical social relationships because I am familiar with the institution involved. Lee Odell's research on self-assessing strategies indicates that employees use their understanding of the corporate hierarchy in revising memos.[5] He also found that low-level personnel were intuitively aware of certain pragmatic principles, even though they had had little or no composition instruction, a finding that suggests that we learn to infer pragmatic characteristics in the process of "learning the ropes" within a particular social setting or institution. While it may be difficult to teach students how to make these inferences outside the context of a particular setting or institution, a teacher can, even within the pragmatic constraints governing "school-writing," show how writers make audience inferences and use those inferences in revising writing.

It is essential that such instruction be based on diagnosis of differences in cognitive and social development that affect the abilities of students to assess their own behavior and to think about audience characteristics. A number of studies have found that the ability of students to infer audience characteristics varies with age.[6] In one of the few studies that defined the relationship between particular writing strategies employed by different age groups and differences in the nature of an audience, Rubin and Piché[7] compared the use of persuasive writing strategies by fourth-, eighth-, and twelfth-graders as well as by expert adult writers according to their familiarity with audience (high versus intermediate versus low intimacy). The older writers, generally twelfth-graders and adults, employed more strategies such as contextualizing than did the younger writers; however, evidence was less clear-cut concerning the extent to which the ability to adapt to audience is developmental.

These studies, however, have not examined the explicit inferences that students make about audience. In my own research, college freshmen composition students judged as either "remedial" or "regular" completed open-ended forms asking them to make inferences about their goals and specific strategies.[8] Content analysis of these forms indicated that the remedial students had much more difficulty in inferring goals, particularly in reference to their audience, than did the regular college freshmen.

An instructor might assess the ability to make inferences about audiences by asking students to complete open-ended forms prior to a rough draft conference. These forms might ask students to make inferences about goals, strategies employed, and audience characteristics. If it is evident from the responses that a student is having difficulty making audience inferences, the instructor could then probe during the conference to determine reasons for the difficulty. In some cases, the student may not have a clear idea about the nature of the topic and may need to do more prewriting before he or she can begin to define audience characteristics. It may also be that the assignment did not make clear who the implied audience was. If the teacher is the audience, the student may not be familiar with the teacher's knowledge or beliefs regarding the topic.

The instructor also needs to assess the ability of students to reflect on their own ideas or those of others. William Perry has defined three levels of cognitive development that are useful for understanding differences in this ability.[9] At Perry's first level, the "dualist" level, students think in concrete categories. Because dualists perceive ideas or knowledge as absolute, they have difficulty entertaining alternative perspectives or understanding that their audience may have a different perspective. Because they see ideas as self-evident, they may not perceive the need to revise their writing in order to substantiate their ideas. They may also be unable to assume the perspective of their audience. Students thinking at the "multiplicity" level recognize multiple perspectives but assume that ideas are equally valid and, therefore, not subject to further evaluation. If "everyone has the right to their own opinion," then students thinking at this level may perceive little dissonance between their own and an audience's beliefs and thus are unaware of the need to revise. Students at the highest level, the "relativistic" level, assume that knowledge is relative to context and are able to entertain multiple perspectives. They are, therefore, willing to evaluate, accept, and incorporate an audience's potential feedback and to perceive the need for revision.

Perry's levels of cognitive development do seem related to the ability to revise. In my own research, revisions on three assignments for 94 twelfth-graders were rated on seven "degree-of-improvement" scales.[10] These students also completed the Conceptual Level Scale developed by D. E. Hunt, a measure of characteristics similar to those defined by Perry.[11] Students who scored high on the Hunt scale revised at a level that was significantly higher on the degree-of-improvement scales than did students who scored low on the Hunt scale.

Based on these observations of the self-assessing abilities of students, I've devised several teaching techniques that might be used to improve the ability of students to self-assess.

Writing assignments. In devising writing assignments, teachers should build in audience characteristics or, ideally, ask students to choose topics and define their own audiences. Teachers might also write "cases" that define specific hypothetical situations. Students can then discuss reasons for making certain inferences about their audience, making explicit the assumptions they made in the process, somewhat as I have done in my discussion of the "fieldhouse memo."

Analyzing texts. Students can read a variety of written materials and discuss purposes, strategies employed, and audience characteristics implied. In responding to these materials, teachers and students model inference processes for students who have difficulty making inferences. Students can also discuss disparities between their own responses as audiences and those of other audiences. They can begin by discussing materials that have familiar audiences, perhaps a memo from the dean to their instructor, determining how accurately the dean perceived the instructor's knowledge or beliefs. They might then discuss how they were able to infer audience characteristics from texts. The fact that a writer uses certain strategies—backgrounding, supporting, defining—suggests that the writer has inferred certain characteristics.

Students might then write memos to each other and discuss the accuracy of their inferences about each other. If they discover disparities between their assumptions about their audience's knowledge and beliefs and their audience's actual knowledge and beliefs, they can discuss ways of adjusting their conceptions and making appropriate revisions.

Modeling assessing behavior. Teacher/student conferences are an ideal opportunity for students to learn self-assessing strategies because the instructor can pose questions designed to elicit inferences about purpose and about audience characteristics. If a student has difficulty making these inferences, the teacher can model the inference process. Because the teacher often serves as the audience for a student's writing, the teacher can make explicit his or her knowledge or beliefs about the paper's topic. The student can then be asked how he or she would use that information in writing or revising the paper.

Formulating criteria for judging discourse. Students can discuss instances of the success or failure of everyday social discourse or fictional dialogue and then make explicit the criteria they used to judge success or failure. They may inductively derive certain principles that are similar to those of Grice. They can then be asked to suggest how those principles might be used to judge their own writing or the writing of others.

Posing challenges to students at the dualist or multiplicity levels. Students who conceive of ideas as absolute and self-evident can be asked to state their opinions. The instructor can then pose challenges that encourage students to consider other perspectives as well as the need to support their opinions. Students who assume that every opinion is equally valid may be challenged by citing counter-evidence that forces them to consider other opinions that they may come to recognize as more valid than their original opinions.

Instructors, of course, must accept the fact that certain students will not change their thinking habits during a given course, or even during a lifetime. By assessing a student's consistent thought processes, however, a writing instructor does at least determine a developmental explanation for that student's difficulties. The central purpose for all these activities is to teach students to assess their own writing. As students become more confident and able to evaluate their writing in terms of pragmatic considerations, they are also learning to revise.

Notes

1. Richard Beach, "Self-Evaluation Strategies of Extensive Revisers and Nonrevisers," *College Composition and Communication* 27 (May 1976): 160–64.

2. E. D. Hirsch, Jr., *The Philosophy of Composition* (Chicago: University of Chicago Press, 1977).

3. H. Paul Grice, "Logic and Conversation," in *Syntax and Semantics: Speech Acts,* vol. 3, eds. Peter Cole and Jerry L. Morgan (New York: Academic Press, Harcourt Brace Jovanovich, 1975), pp. 45–46.

4. William Labov and David Fanshell, *Therapeutic Discourse* (New York: Academic Press, 1977).

5. Lee Odell, "Writing in the Real World" (Paper presented at the convention of the National Council of Teachers of English, San Francisco, November 1979).

6. See, for example, Robert Bracewell, Marlene Scardamalia, and Carl Bereiter, "The Development of Audience Awareness in Writing" (Paper presented at the meeting of the American Educational Research Association, Toronto, March 1978, ERIC Document Reproduction Service No. ED 154 433); and Barry M. Kroll, "Cognitive Egocentrism and the Problem of Audience Awareness in Written Discourse," *Research in the Teaching of English* 12 (October 1978): 269–81.

7. Donald L. Rubin and Gene L. Piché, "Development in Syntactic and Strategic Aspects of Audience Adaptation Skills in Written Persuasive Communication," *Research in the Teaching of English* 13 (December 1979): 293–316.

8. Richard Beach, "The Self-assessing Strategies of Remedial College Students" (Paper presented at the meeting of the American Educational Research Association, Boston, April 1980).

9. William Perry, Jr., *Intellectual and Ethical Development in the College Years* (New York: Holt, Rinehart, and Winston, 1970).

10. Richard Beach, "The Effects of Teacher Assessment on Students' Self-assessing and Revising" (Paper presented at the convention of the National Council of Teachers of English, San Francisco, November 1979).

11. David E. Hunt, "A Conceptual Level Matching Model for Coordinating Learning Characteristics with Educational Approaches," *Interchange,* May 1970, pp. 68–82.

Application: Contexts and Techniques

A Holistic Pedagogy for Freshman Composition

Ruth Windhover
University of Idaho

The need for new paradigms in the study and teaching of writing has recently become apparent.[1] We have found that the old paradigms, drawn primarily from analytic, knowledge-oriented models of literary study and teaching, do not fit the process- and skills-oriented discipline of writing. We have also found that our knowledge of kinds of discourse other than literary discourse is limited, and that the application of many of our assumptions about literary discourse to other types is faulty. Researchers, therefore, have begun to observe writers writing and to examine a variety of types of contemporary discourse. Such observation has shown the weakness of a model that segments the composing process into prewriting, writing, and rewriting.[2] When researchers watch people write, they find that unless the writers are very experienced or the writing situation is simple and familiar, the process is generally a recursive one in which revision begins immediately and invention may occur in the final stages.[3] Further, successful writers rely on a holistic concept in preparing to invent and revise, concentrating on parts during the process of writing. Since the process does not have discrete segments, a theory or pedagogy of rewriting must be one of prewriting and writing as well.

I will begin this discussion by explaining how the assumptions on which it is based differ from established ones.

Teachers traditionally see a writing assignment as a "topic" to write about; students come up with "things to say" about that topic until they hit upon a generalization under which a number of their "things to say" can be subsumed. In contrast, recent rhetorical theory suggests the greater power of viewing a writing assignment, in or out of the classroom, as a problem to be solved.[4] This problem grows out of what Lloyd Bitzer has called a rhetorical situation,[5] which the successful writer investigates by analyzing and describing its aspects—writer, audience, subject, and exigence. These descriptions then act as constraints to guide the writer's response.

Traditionally, writing instructors intervene at the end of the writing process, focus on the finished product, and respond at the same time to all types of problems—from basic organizational weaknesses to spelling errors. Their comments may suggest revision strategies, but error-based responses after students have handed in drafts they consider finished often result only in minor revisions. Empirical studies show, however, that even inexperienced writers consciously use strategies, however weak and ineffective they may be. Researchers have developed methods to identify and improve these strategies, enabling instructors to intervene both before and during the writing process.[6] Such intervention enables teachers to respond hierarchically and, by using common assignments, to teach the strategies to the class rather than to individual students.

Traditional writing instruction has also concentrated on a general, abstract concept of "good writing," which instructors often illustrate with the writing of professionals. Most freshman composition texts contain models that differ greatly in subject, purpose, audience, style, or complexity from the writing students are trying to produce. Most freshmen, however, lack the generalizing power to abstract from these models general features that they can incorporate into their own work, or to construct strategies for producing them.

A student can use a model if he or she is taught to see it as a solution to a particular kind of writing problem, just as experienced writers use knowledge of the typical form and content of a particular genre when they write in that genre. Linda Flower and John R. Hayes posit that experienced writers categorize a new writing problem as a variation of a familiar problem. To solve it, they draw on information in a "stored problem representation," which may contain "not only a conventional definition of the situation, audience, and the writer's purpose, but might include quite detailed information about solutions, even down to appropriate tone and phrases. Experienced writers are likely to have stored representations of even quite complex rhetorical problems (e.g., writing a book review for readers of *The Daily Tribune*) if they have confronted them often before."[7]

Given these assumptions about the process of writing and its teaching, let us examine some empirical studies of successful and unsuccessful writers. Flower and Hayes compared the strategies that novice and professional writers use in constructing a writing

problem. After giving the fairly unelaborated and unusual assignment, "Write about your job for the readers of *Seventeen* magazine, thirteen- and fourteen-year-old girls," Flower and Hayes
observed that expert writers first built for themselves their own
representation of the rhetorical situation and then constructed
goals for their writing. The four dominant kinds of goals, "affect-
ing the *reader,* creating a *persona* or voice, building a *meaning,*
and producing a formal *text*" parallel the aspects of the communication triangle—writer, subject, and audience—and the mediator
among them, language.[8] Flower and Hayes note that "one of the
most telling differences between our good and poor writers was
the degree to which they created a unique, fully-developed representation of this unique rhetorical problem."[9] For example, thinking about the characteristics of their readers helped the good
writers to invent; for them "setting up goals to affect a reader"
was "a powerful strategy for generating new ideas and exploring
even a topic as personal as 'my job.'"[10] Novice writers, however,
did not try to elaborate the rhetorical situation implicit in the
assignment to help them invent, but rather simply reread the
assignment "as if searching for a clue." They never "moved
beyond the sketchy, conventional representation of audience and
assignment with which they started."[11]

Studies of revision strategies show that good writers construct
holistic goals like those they use to invent. Nancy I. Sommers
found that good writers conceptualize the effect of their draft as
a whole when they revise, seeing as their main concern "finding
a framework, a pattern, or a design for their argument," and
beginning to observe "general patterns of development and deciding what should be included and what excluded."[12] They revise
in cycles, attending primarily but not exclusively to specific concerns in each one. In an earlier study, "Self-Evaluation Strategies
of Extensive Revisers and Nonrevisers," Richard Beach found
similar results.[13] College juniors and seniors who revised extensively "were able to generalize about different aspects of their
drafts, because they tended to conceive of the paper in holistic
terms. . . . [They] inferred general patterns of development or
major ideas and then evaluated those patterns and ideas on an
abstract level."[14] This ability to generalize helped them to use
such information from a first draft as the cause of and solution
to a problem to improve subsequent drafts.

The poor writers and nonrevisers in both of these studies tended
to use nonholistic strategies. The college freshmen Sommers observed saw revision as a process of rewording, not one of adding

new ideas discovered while writing. Repetition of words was their primary cue for revising, but they seemed unaware of conceptual repetition in their writing. Other cues were violations of such rules as the prohibition against beginning a sentence with a conjunction. Sommers concludes that poor writers make few revisions because they "do not see revision as an activity on the idea level, and because they feel that . . . they must know before writing what they want to say."[15] Even if they attain a holistic perspective on a writing problem, they often lack revising strategies, as a typical comment shows: "'I knew something larger was wrong, but I didn't think it would help to move words around.'"[16]

Beach also found that nonrevisers saw revising as the making of "minor alterations in matters of form" rather than major alterations of substance. He reports that nonrevisers "would read aloud sentences or sections of a draft and simply describe or explain their choices, assuming that their writing needed no revision. Once they had described or judged matters of form, noting that their wording was 'awkward,' 'trite,' or 'vivid,' they were satisfied that they had completed their evaluation, as if the process of labeling was an end in itself."[17] Nonrevisers often "assumed that once they had expressed their thoughts [in freewriting], there was little need for further major reworking," whereas revisers saw freewriting as "a spontaneous, tentative record of their thoughts that would need to be . . . reformulated."[18] Nonrevisers saw problems as part of a "checklist" and concentrated on such minor matters as the "sound" or "look" of words and phrases.

In summary, good writers seem to do the following:

1. analyze and elaborate the rhetorical situation, using a description of writer, audience, purpose and subject to invent
2. set particular goals for the writing and formulate strategies for achieving them
3. draw on past experience with similar rhetorical situations and similar rhetorical forms (i.e., a personal narrative, an objective analysis) to construct a model for what their writing should look like, making appropriate modifications to meet the unique features of the situation
4. write, referring back to the guides in the first three steps
5. view their writing holistically, as readers do, recognizing where it does not fit their internalized model of a good response and devising hierarchical strategies to improve it

Finding a pedagogy to teach these writing skills is not easy, since they differ widely in difficulty and complexity. One of the abilities needed to master them seems to be "creativity," the apparently unteachable ability to produce original writing, whether it be a simple personal narrative or a complex allegory. The constructing of clear, readable sentences, on the other hand, seems a craft teachable to most freshmen, as studies of sentence-combining techniques demonstrate. Editing and proofreading seem quasi-mechanical skills that depend on fairly low-level rote memorization and mechanical application.

Those who emphasize the creative aspects of writing favor a "studio" model in which students work independently. Since the essential act of writing is seen as suprarational intuition or inspiration, the teacher cannot intervene, but must be content with setting up an environment conducive to creativity. Often assignments are student-generated; if not, the teacher gives vague assignments in the expressive mode, assignments which have few constraints: "Write about how you feel about nature." The instructor acts as critic of the final product, using originality and truthfulness as criteria. Teachers with the opposing philosophy concentrate on correctness—grammar, punctuation, spelling, and usage—and see the "factory" as the appropriate model. Writing is supplemented, or even supplanted, by exercises and quizzes. Students often write on descriptive and persuasive topics with unelaborated rhetorical situations like, "Describe your room," "Explain how to change a tire," or "The draft: yes or no?" Often readings are assigned to provide content for the papers and external constraints such as the five-paragraph essay form or a length limit are given. The teacher is a kind of "foreman" who sets up the assignment and checks the quality of the results. The primary criterion is conformity.

Although instructors of writing acknowledge the virtue of originality and good grammar, many have rejected these models. Results of the studio model dominant in the 1960s indicate that most freshmen were not very good at coming up with fruitful, sequential rhetorical situations for assignments. Although students often critiqued each other's work in class, devising and applying helpful criteria and strategies were difficult because assignments differed radically and the class hadn't discussed them beforehand. Besides, abstracting the general concepts of "good writing" from a poem wasn't much help to a student who was writing a persuasive letter. The weakness of the studio model is that it uses the goals of a writing class—to have students generate independently their own writing problems, criteria, and strategies—as means. The factory model, on the other hand, seems to deny the complexity of even a simple writing task, and many researchers seriously question whether correctness exercises improve student writing.[19] But because of a variety of factors such as large composition teaching loads, the emphasis of the back-to-basics movement on correctness, the increasing prevalence of objective competency tests, and high-powered marketing by publishers of basic writing materials, the factory model is common. In fact, parts of the model are efficient. Responding to similar assignments is easier and quicker than responding to varied ones, an advantage of the course model proposed in this paper.

The classroom model prevalent in current professional literature is the workshop, an appealing model based on how medieval masters taught similarly complex skills: "The shop was small; master and apprentice often worked side by side at the same bench. The master himself worked at all processes of his handicraft, and therefore it was comparatively easy for him to teach all processes to the lad at his side. It was comparatively easy, too, for the lad to follow all the workings of his master and to imitate them. The number of apprentices being small the master could give each one a large part of his attention."[20]

The workshop model is attractive,[21] but we have more students and less time to spend with them than the medieval master and must look to the factory for more efficient methods. An industrial efficiency expert might advise us not only to standardize our assignments and responses, but also to establish a hierarchy of them and to set up specifications for each writing task that students can use in writing and reviewing their work.

In the freshman writing course I describe in the rest of this paper I try to incorporate this advice without oversimplifying or making mechanical either writing or teaching. This course presumes that freshman writers can learn the fundamentals of writing through common assignments, and that a teacher should concentrate on *common* features and strategies with the entire class. *Individual* instruction, both in written comments and conferences, should be used to help students internalize and use these strategies, not to present them.

The highly constrained, sequenced assignments in this course are based on a thorough description of the role of the writer, the intended audience, and the nature of the subject. An emphasis on one of these aspects leads to determination of purpose and mode:

if the writer is most emphasized, the writing is expressive; if the subject is dominant, the mode is explanatory; a focus on audience results in persuasion. James Kinneavy discusses this model at length;[22] it is also the one used by Richard Lloyd-Jones and others in their development of the primary trait scoring system for the National Assessment of Educational Progress.[23] To generate writing assignments, the instructor selects a topic with which students are familiar and then devises assignments in each mode by emphasizing one of the elements. Students are involved in this process, and toward the end of the course may begin to devise their own assignments. If, for example, the topic is jobs and the focus is on the writer, the assignment might be to write about a particularly enjoyable feature; the purpose would be expression, and the reader might be a parent or friend. If the focus were on the job itself, students might write a descriptive guide for doing the job, perhaps for workers to be hired when the writers left. The audience would be specific although not personally known, and the purpose would be to explain the major duties of the job explicitly and sequentially so a reader could learn how to do them. Assignments that focus on audience might include a letter of complaint concerning working conditions, a letter of recommendation for a friend, a letter to convince a friend to apply for a job, or a memo requesting a raise. In each case, the purpose is to persuade a reader to act.

The basic assignment is given in class, and discussion follows on how to develop the assignment into a particular rhetorical problem. Students write in the same form and use similar content but invent their own specifics. After they understand the rhetorical situation, they need a concept of what the essential features of a successful response are and strategies for achieving these features. Primary trait scoring techniques are adapted for this purpose.

In generating primary traits, NAEP scorers examine a number of responses to a particular writing assignment and identify those traits common to all successful responses. In a scoring guide they rate these features for their presence and, usually, for their quality. For example, the primary trait of an exercise that asks writers to respond expressively to a picture was "Imaginative Expression of Feeling through Inventive Elaboration of a *Point of View.*"[24] Scores were given for the entire exercise, and for the criteria of dialogue, point of view, and tense. A "0" was given if the feature was absent, undeterminable, or uncontrolled, and a "1," "2," or "3," depending on how the feature was treated.

Lloyd-Jones explains that "expressive prose often was described in terms of the kinds of responses made—not presuming, for example, that either categorical or associative organizational systems were to be preferred, or even that lots of concrete detail was self-evidently better than well-knit abstractions. Simply, the score points indicated what the writer did." However, he notes, "Most of the guides of persuasive or referential writing use numbers (scores) which indicate a value placed on the observed performances."[25] In a scoring guide to a persuasive piece on "Woman's Place," for instance, a response which "takes a position and gives one unelaborated reason" received two points; one which "takes a position and gives one elaborated reason, one elaborated plus one unelaborated reason, or two or three unelaborated reasons" received three points. The guide also provides points for the presence of various appeals (conventional wisdom, personal experience, etc.) and for their use (advanced in own cause, offered to refute opposing position, etc.).[26]

Since primary trait scoring was developed for evaluation, it is concerned with the written product. However, the scorers are also interested in getting the best writing possible from the writers they test, so they build into the assignments a number of constraints to help the writers. Learning to recognize and develop these constraints and the traits of a good response helps students know what to do (i.e., take a position) and how to do it (i.e., use a personal experience to advance your cause). For example, in a letter recommending a friend for a job the writer has held, the purpose is to persuade a specific employer to hire a specific person for a specific job. A primary trait of all good letters is the demonstration that the person recommended has the desired characteristics. Another primary trait is the establishment of the writer as a credible recommender who knows and can speak about the person's qualifications. Secondary traits, which suggest strategies, include the use of details to show not only general qualifications but also specific ones that set the candidate apart from others and the use of formal diction to set a tone appropriate to the reader-writer relationship, even when the situation being described is informal.

Identifying an assignment as an example of a particular kind of discourse helps testmakers know what an accurate and adequate response to it is. Lloyd-Jones cites a letter from students to their principal suggesting an improvement to the school as an example of discourse "fairly close to the line between explanatory and persuasive discourse, closer to the persuasive end." However, he continues, "If parents were the audience, we might posit that a larger expressive dimension would be appropriate, and we might consider that the usefulness of wheedling would push the exercise closer to pure persuasion."[27] He points out the procedures most teachers use in making assignments: "We imagine that most teachers practiced in creating classroom exercises will also create the situation first. Then they can analyze the rhetorical implications, placing the exercise on the model; this will serve as an aid in discovering the features which characterize writing in the prescribed mode."[28] Making students aware of the mode of each assignment helps them build a repertory of related invention, writing, and revising strategies to use in writing in a particular mode or for a particular purpose. Teachers can carefully sequence common assignments so that students can use strategies and forms developed for early assignments in writing later ones. Persuasive assignments, for instance, typically incorporate expressive and/or explanatory passages to achieve their purpose. In writing a letter of recommendation, students might recall the kinds of specifics they used in writing a description of the requirements of their job. Both are problems of presenting and describing job-related characteristics, but the letter adds a persuasive element not present in the description.

To determine primary traits is not easy, even for experienced writers. The NAEP scorers examined a large number of responses before they were able to formulate accurate, reliable traits. The first time a teacher makes an assignment, he or she has no student responses to examine with the class. In this case teacher and students may predict the traits of a successful response and the strategies for achieving them. Drawing on the class's common experience of previous writing can be useful, and traits may also be revised in progress as a result of looking at first drafts. Then, too, teachers can write model responses themselves, and demonstration writing, which I will discuss later on, is an important aspect in my freshman writing course. Another useful strategy is for upper-level students to write on these assignments, since their writing generally provides significantly better models than freshmen writing does. Yet it is easier for freshmen to "indwell" in the work of other students than in that of professionals. Since students need to understand the model in the same way that they understand the rhetorical situation, class discussion should analyze the model as communication by a particular person to a particular audience about a particular subject for a particular purpose.

A model, then, should help students both to know what a successful response looks like and how to achieve it. When the instructor writes models for the class, students can see how experienced writers formulate and devise strategies. Students also learn, through observation and imitation, behaviors of competent writers which recent empirical studies have shown to be significant, behaviors like pausing to reread portions of the text or simply to reflect.[29] Yet teachers often fail to teach these behaviors because they don't use them consciously (as Michael Polanyi explains, "We can know more than we can tell"[30]), because they don't realize the relationship of the behaviors to good writing, or because they assume that students already practice them. Demonstrations of students writing are also useful. Successful students may write for the class, and the instructor may observe a student writing during a conference or tape and analyze a student's writing protocol.[31] All these methods concentrate on describing and improving writing strategies.

Elaborating the assignment, examining models, watching the teacher or other students write, and formulating traits all give students criteria and strategies to help them invent, write, and revise. If students list these criteria and strategies in their pre-draft writing, which they hand in with their draft, responding teachers can refer to them easily without need for discussion or explanation. Thus teacher response can be limited to brief, particular advice for the next major task the student should work on. Since the traits form a hierarchy, so does teacher response. Successful writers have different primary concerns at each step. For example, they usually concentrate on organization and development before explicit transitions, sentence structure, and diction, and concern for these elements logically precedes concern for correctness features like proper grammar, punctuation, and spelling. At the first two levels a teacher should comment holistically from the point of view of the intended audience and then suggest particular strategies for the next stage of development. When a paper successfully meets the assignment's rhetorical and stylistic demands, the teacher responds to problems of correctness by analyzing their causes.

A practical result of this approach is to make a writing teacher's evaluation criteria hierarchical and explicit and to assure that students understand the nature and purpose of these criteria. Lloyd-Jones comments, "A user of the test can easily examine just what the testers thought they were examining. The test thus gains credibility in its openness. Not the authority of the reader but the persuasiveness of the scoring guide becomes the issue."[32]

Establishing criteria for revision before students begin to write also discourages them from viewing writing as the transcription of an unconscious flow of ideas and revising as the cleaning up of surface errors of this transcription.

The course may seem too close to the factory model, for freshmen are not at the beginning of the course capable of constructing and elaborating rhetorical situations, nor do they have adequate stored problem representations to help them write discourse of the length and complexity required for college work. In fact, students initially may write fairly close imitations of the models, using them as frameworks for sentence- or even phrase-level substitutions. Such practice helps students who become paralyzed when confronted with a writing assignment—a larger group than we generally realize. Responses to early assignments also may be as short as 200–300 words, for brevity helps students gain a holistic grasp of models and of their own writing.

As students internalize revision strategies, they write better and longer first drafts and handle more constraints and more aspects of revision simultaneously. Teachers can then encourage students to assume greater responsibility for revising by grading certain assignments that are similar to ones students have previously worked on and discussed in class but that have not had the benefit of teacher response and subsequent revision. If students continue to imitate models too closely after having mastered the skills of a particular level of assignment, the models may be passed out, discussed, and then collected.

The assignments also move toward greater length and complexity by increasing the distance between writer and reader and between writer and subject, and by dealing with increasingly complex subject matter and forms (i.e., beginning with a thank-you note to a relative and moving to a letter persuading a member of Congress to support a bill). Although assignments, especially early ones, specify constraints fairly strictly, students have flexibility in elaborating their aspects. Lloyd-Jones reports that the NAEP writings yield "many quite legitimate solutions which we had not imagined. We were delighted by the inventiveness of respondents and quickly learned that even highly structured situations permit a variety of appropriate responses."[33]

Early assignments may seem undemanding because they rely only on student experience and do not require students to incorporate new information into their writing. For students unskilled in rhetorical principles, however, to identify and incorporate new information successfully, as well as to retrieve and shape familiar information, is extremely difficult. Drawing on their own experience may also give students confidence and motivation. Lloyd-Jones reports, for example, that test-givers elicit cooperation from writers in part by giving them a satisfying task, and "knowledge of the subject is part of the satisfaction."[34]

The main concern of the course is that students achieve a holistic view of a writing problem as they begin to write and that they learn to view their own writing holistically so they can make major revisions in it. Paradoxically, to gain this holistic perspective requires concentrating on a limited number of the essential traits of the writing problem and of the writing itself. But as Lloyd-Jones explains, "To some extent one must know less to know more. A sharper focus eliminates some of the penumbra of a general skill, but it gives a sharper view of the complex of particular skills required to do a given task, and therefore increases the likelihood that we will be able to identify strengths and weaknesses precisely."[35] To do so is certainly one of the most important skills that a writer can possess and that a writing instructor can teach.

Notes

1. See, for example, Richard E. Young, "Paradigms and Problems: Needed Research in Rhetorical Invention," in *Research on Composing: Points of Departure,* eds. Charles R. Cooper and Lee Odell (Urbana, Ill.: National Council of Teachers of English, 1978), pp. 29–47.

2. See Nancy I. Sommers's reassessment of a linear theory of the composing process in "The Need for Theory in Composition Research," *College Composition and Communication* 30 (February 1979): 46–49.

3. See, for example, Nancy I. Sommers, "Revision Strategies of Student Writers and Experienced Writers" (Paper presented at the annual meeting of the Modern Language Association, December 28, 1978).

4. Richard E. Young, Alton L. Becker, and Kenneth L. Pike discuss at length the concept of writing-as-problem-solving in *Rhetoric: Discovery and Change* (New York: Harcourt Brace Jovanovich, 1970), especially chapters 5–7.

5. Lloyd Bitzer defines and discusses the concept in "The Rhetorical Situation," *Philosophy and Rhetoric* 1 (January 1968): 1–14.

6. John R. Hayes and Linda S. Flower, for instance, study the writing process using protocol analysis, a technique adapted from cognitive psychology, in "Identifying the Organization of Writing Processes," Xerox copy, Carnegie-Mellon University.

7. Linda Flower and John R. Hayes, "The Cognition of Discovery: Defining a Rhetorical Problem," *College Composition and Communication* 31 (February 1980): 25.

8. Ibid., p. 25.

9. Ibid.

10. Ibid., p. 30.

11. Ibid., p. 26.

12. Sommers, "Revision Strategies," p. 7.

13. Richard Beach, "Self-Evaluation Strategies of Extensive Revisers and Nonrevisers," *College Composition and Communication* 27 (May 1976): 160-64.

14. Ibid., p. 162.

15. Sommers, "Revision Strategies," p. 5.

16. Ibid., p. 6.

17. Beach, p. 161.

18. Ibid., p. 162.

19. J. Stephen Sherwin, *Four Problems in Teaching English: A Critique of Research* (Scranton, Pa.: International Textbook Co., 1969).

20. Jonathan F. Scott, *Historical Essays on Apprenticeship and Vocational Education* (Ann Arbor, Mich.: Ann Arbor Press, 1914), pp. 51-52.

21. Ruth Mitchell and Mary Taylor construct three similar models in "The Integrating Perspective: An Audience-Response Model for Writing," *College English* 41 (November 1979): 247-71. They define these models by a major emphasis on writer, product, or audience. Their "writer" model corresponds to the studio model, their "product" model to the factory model, and their "audience-response" model to the workshop.

22. James Kinneavy, *A Theory of Discourse* (Englewood Cliffs, N.J.: Prentice-Hall, 1971).

23. For a full explanation of the primary trait scoring system, see Richard Lloyd-Jones, "Primary Trait Scoring," in *Evaluating Writing: Describing, Measuring, Judging,* eds. Charles R. Cooper and Lee Odell (Urbana, Ill.: National Council of Teachers of English, 1977), pp. 33-66. Professor Gene H. Krupa, former Director of Composition, incorporated primary trait scoring and the method of generating assignments described in this paper into the first of two freshman writing courses at the University of Idaho. See his article, "Primary Trait Scoring in the Classroom," *College Composition and Communication* 30 (May 1979): 214-15.

24. Lloyd-Jones, p. 48.

25. Ibid., p. 45.

26. Ibid., pp. 62-66.

27. Ibid., p. 42.

28. Ibid.

29. See, for example, Sharon Pianko, "Reflection: A Critical Component of the Composing Process," *College Composition and Communication* 30 (October 1979): 275-78.

30. *The Tacit Dimension* (New York: Doubleday, 1966), p. 4.

31. Peter M. Schiff discusses some of these strategies in "Revising the Writing Conference," *College Composition and Communication* 29 (October 1978): 294-96.

32. Lloyd-Jones, p. 47.

33. Lloyd-Jones, p. 45.

34. Lloyd-Jones, p. 43.

35. Lloyd-Jones, p. 47.

Teaching Teachers
to Teach Revision

Toby Fulwiler
Michigan Technological University

The act of revision is the operational core of the composing process. Revision bridges the gap between one stage of creation and the next. Few of us who learned to teach writing under the tutelage of Ken Macrorie, Donald Murray, or James Moffett doubt this. We studied carefully each stage of revision—prewriting, writing, rewriting, editing—and tried to teach this process to our students.

At the same time, many of us were discouraged because our students seldom paid the same homage to revision that we did. All too often, students in first-year composition and fourth-year literature alike believed that revision meant shuffling around a few commas on last night's paper before handing it in. While this generalization does disservice to serious student writers, it remains true for many who completed our classes with far less language proficiency than we had hoped for. In other cases, students who were apt and able writers in our writing classes became loose and careless in literature and philosophy classes. The lessons didn't stick.

I remain convinced, however, that Macrorie, Murray, and Moffett are right and that my own instruction is sound. Too much other stuff just gets in the way. An eighteen-year-old freshman, for example, is more concerned with untying Mom's apron strings, getting to know his roommate, dating, and choosing a major than he is in honing and polishing his writing skills. In like manner, a junior or senior concentrates her academic energy on her major and pays less attention to electives; fewer and fewer majors during the 1970s were in English. Older students with experience in the world of work know that writing is serious business; they have learned that literate people get good jobs and fast promotions. But most of our undergraduates do not have this seasoned perspective and consequently continue to treat writing instruction as more hurdle than help.

We *do know* how to teach writing in our writing classes, but the lessons do not last because we cannot teach motivation. That needs to come from somewhere else. We need an academic equivalent to the employment imperative that motivates older students, one that functions at the undergraduate level. I believe that such help can come from colleagues who teach subjects other than English. Teachers in the student's major department are far closer to the student's prospective world of work than are English teachers. Nor do sociology or business teachers suffer from the same long-term stigmas as English teachers who have too faithfully red-penciled misspelled words on student compositions all the student's life; students do not view teachers in other disciplines as they view English teachers—"hung up" on correct language. ("I better watch my grammar.")

The problem at many universities is the absence of a comprehensive literate environment that encourages, reinforces, teaches, and demands good language habits—including reading and speaking as well as writing. Without such an environment, there is little pressure on students to take writing seriously. ("Why should I care—my major professor doesn't.") In other words, if the lessons we teach in writing classes are not reinforced in the student's other classes, those lessons will not be learned. We must share with our colleagues what we teach to our students. If chemistry and physics teachers are not aware that revision is the core of the writing process, then we must teach them that. In the final analysis, we are all teachers of language.

This essay offers some suggestions for teaching teachers in all disciplines how to nourish and encourage good writing habits among their students. Most teachers know experientially and intuitively that revision is necessary for good writing; at the same time these teachers seldom give writing assignments that reflect that tacit knowledge. Their understanding of writing has not been translated into classroom pedagogy. A few teachers insist that writing is strictly the business of English teachers; however, most teachers simply have not thought about teaching writing nor have they felt confident enough to teach it. English teachers, as professional students of writing, need to show their colleagues just how much they already do know and how to put that knowledge into classroom practice. Such a program, which James Britton calls "writing across the curriculum," actively promotes literacy in the campus community.

The best way to develop a writing-across-the-curriculum program is to conduct intensive writing workshops for faculty members from all disciplines. Together with a codirector, I invite

twenty teachers to travel in university automobiles to an off-
season resort for two to four days of talking about writing,
examining writing, and doing writing. We discuss the problems
they most frequently encounter with student writing and solicit
suggestions for curing those problems. Finally, we conduct carefully structured exercises to make participants aware of the complex, multifaceted nature of the composing process. In particular,
we demonstrate that writing serves at least two distinct and
different functions for mature human beings—facilitating communication and aiding learning. Revision is critical to both functions, involving as it does rewriting and rethinking. What follows
is a brief description of three workshop activities that stress
different parts of the revision process.

Journal Writing

Participants at the writing workshop keep journals throughout
the workshop and at the end of the first day discuss among themselves the value of writing in journals. This discussion takes place
only after they have written a dozen journal entries during the
first day. James Britton and his colleagues have argued that
informal, personal "expressive writing" helps writers discover
what they have to say, organize and clarify existing ideas, and
initiate written projects, proposals, and papers.[1] In other words,
expressive writing in journals is a process of thinking as well as
a record of thought—a means and an end of creation at the same
time.

By itself the journal is a personal revision workshop, a place
where writers can carry on dialogues with themselves in order
to find out what to write, how to write it, and how to modify and
edit what is written. A journal provides a place within a single
document to record flashy insights, tentative plans, trial outlines,
and scratchy first drafts of a piece of writing. A writer who carefully develops the habit of journal writing acquires a tool useful
in all phases of professional and academic work. I do not understand why journal writing in college remains primarily in the
domain of English teachers; once exposed to the idea of journals,
most teachers see immediately the possibilities of using them for
themselves and for their students.

At the writing workshop we insist that our colleagues give
journals a rigorous trial by asking them to complete a variety
of writing tasks in their journals. In particular, we ask them to
complete the following:

1. Summarize a particular workshop lesson or discussion and give it written shape. This activity both organizes the event for the writer and provides a written record of the ideas or information.

2. Anticipate a discussion topic by answering a question in their journals. A typical question might be, "What problem do you perceive with student writing?" The journal entries then become the direct subject matter for the next hour's discussion.

3. Clarify a difficult concept central to the work at hand. By asking participants to write out their understanding of Britton's concept of "expressive writing," for example, I can be sure that they have grappled with the notion internally before we conclude a discussion of the idea.

4. Interrupt a heated or confused discussion in order to refocus. In this sense, writing in their journals serves as a "time out" for the whole group, as it would for a class of students, and lets individuals rethink where the group ought to go from here.

5. "Freewrite" for a specified period of time as a way of beginning a piece of writing. Using Peter Elbow's definition of free-association writing,[2] I ask participants to write rapidly for ten minutes on a given topic—"one memorable experience you have had with writing." The journal is a place in which to practice freewriting and to keep permanent records of it.

6. Brainstorm in order to invent new ideas. For example, participants can be asked to discover as many possible uses for journals in their classrooms as they can in ten minutes of writing. This heuristic is useful, later, in helping students find topics to write about.

7. Record personal impressions of the workshop: What is my role in the discussions? How do I feel being asked to write on command? How could this workshop be improved? In other words, each participant's thoughts remain confidentially recorded in the journal.

8. Review the workshop experience. On the last day I ask participants to index their journals: number the pages, reread each entry, make a title page. This exercise causes journal writers to reflect consciously on both the worth of the journal and their personal experience of the workshop. (I ask students to do this same activity at the end of a term in all courses I teach.)

It is seldom necessary for me to explain the classroom possibilities of journals after participants have spent several days
writing in them. Participants often take turns suggesting ideas
relevant to their particular discipline. Once the discussion reaches
this point, a corner has been turned. Questions no longer arise
about the value of journals but about how to use them; teachers
want to know how to give directions for keeping journals, whether
or not to collect and read them, and how to evaluate journals
as part of the student's course work. Sometimes I ask the participants to suggest answers to these questions; at other times I
explain options for handling journals used by teachers I know.

The journal-writing exercises serve more than one purpose at a
faculty workshop—just as they do when assigned in a classroom.
Journals teach teachers the value of personal writing as a way
to knowledge as well as a critical step in the revision process; this
perception may influence both their professional writing and how
they teach their classes. In addition, journal writing increases
participation at the workshop because it asks people to write out
their thoughts prior to speaking—teachers, like students, are more
relaxed when prepared. The workshop leaders can also use these
brief writing periods to organize their thoughts about the progress
of the workshop and to consider changes that might improve it.

Journal writing allows writers to watch themselves think and
to try things out. Journals contain scraps of thought in chronological order; when a writer reviews a journal, some of the scraps
may begin to make whole sense—or suggest a further thought
that is more complete. The journal is a place for a writer to review and rethink his or her thinking, which is the essence of
substantive revision. Journals also can be places to try out new
voices, different rhetorical stances, or a particular style. In other
words, journals are places in which to practice both the content
and form of a piece of writing.

Journal writing promotes revision implicitly, by making the
writer a legitimate and important audience, and explicitly, by re-
taining in writing a reviewable record of speculation, exploration,
and discovery. Teachers in a wide variety of disciplines tell me
that assigning journals makes it easy and natural to teach the
process of revision to their students. The first step, however, is
convincing teachers to try it themselves.

Responding to Writing

Workshop participants are asked to respond individually and
collectively to a piece of student writing. They begin by reading

silently a student paper and examining it for strengths and weaknesses, which they jot down in the margin. This activity demands that they add a positive focus to their naturally critical eyes.

Next, participants are grouped in threes and asked to generate a consensus response to the student that will help in rewriting the paper. To do this they must compare ideas and roughly agree on a common vocabulary. It does not matter which terms are used, so long as all understand them; for instance, if one teacher says a paper "lacks focus," another that it "wanders," and a third that it has "no thesis," they understand each other and can communicate to the rest of us—or to the student. No limits are placed on the *kind* of response—written, oral, taped—that teachers might make. The process used by the teachers to arrive at a response is probably more important than the response itself. Many times they find out that others in their group share a similar point of view; at the same time, their own perspective is often broadened and validated. Working together, teachers gain confidence that they are capable of making significant, helpful comments to student writers.

Finally, I ask each group to outline briefly its response on the board. We then compare outlines, noting similarities and differences. The list commonly includes comments on thesis statement, mechanics, style, logic, and organization, together with recommendations about oral conferences, the value of praise, and suggestions for rewriting and grading. It is important for the workshop leader to be descriptive rather than prescriptive, and to highlight the places where teachers agree most. There is not, after all, a "right" or "wrong" response, so much as more or less helpful responses—and what is helpful to one student might not be to another.

In spite of a good measure of subjectivity, a common list of suggestions always emerges that, in fact, is likely to help the majority of students. Teachers who think hard about helping student writers usually develop strategies that involve some form of positive reinforcement, revision, and individual conference. At the end of the workshop, participants will have compiled a guideline for responding to student writing similar to the following:

1. Point out strengths as well as weaknesses in each paper handed back.

2. Focus on one or two problems at a time rather than insisting that students learn and correct everything in one draft.

3. Be specific when commenting about what is wrong; what, exactly, can a student do to make the paper better?

4. Rather than grading poor papers, ask that they be rewritten, for that strategy ensures that the learning process continues.

5. Set up oral conferences with students whose writing poses special problems; in the long run one-to-one instruction can save time for student and teacher.

Since most teachers value revision, it is natural for them to feel comfortable teaching it—once they understand the truly critical importance it plays in the learning process; never has a group suggested flunking the student who wrote the paper under consideration and moving on to the next project. This activity is a strong affirmation of common sense applied to writing instruction, for though most teachers know the value of rewriting prior to the workshop, many have routinely ignored it when evaluating the prose of their own students. A principle such as this, made conscious through group discussion, encourages individual teachers to comment more carefully on student papers. ("I do know some things about teaching writing!") When teachers witness common sense practiced by colleagues and affirmed by writing teachers, some of the mystique about teaching writing necessarily vanishes—which is what we want to happen.

The Composing Process

At a writing workshop participants must write—not only in private journals, but also in a public mode to share with colleagues. It is possible even at a two-day workshop for participants to generate a piece of writing through a journal entry, revise it with an audience in mind, receive feedback, revise it again, and create a relatively final draft. This compressed version of the composing process places faculty members in the role of student, creating personal anxiety on the one hand and increased empathy for student writers on the other.

First, each participant "freewrites" on a common topic: "Write about one memorable writing experience you have had—good or bad, love letter or dissertation." Again following Peter Elbow's advice, I ask them to write as rapidly as they can for ten minutes. ("Do not stop your pen from moving. Do not worry about spelling or punctuation.") The purpose is to get everyone in the room to generate at least a page of copy so that serious rewriting can follow. (To lend credibility, the workshop leader should participate in this activity along with the group.)

Second, each participant spends twenty minutes revising this piece of writing in preparation to sharing it with someone else in the room. ("Expand, edit, clarify, cut, focus—do whatever is necessary to make this piece of freewriting a piece of transactional writing aimed at an audience outside yourself.")

Third, in an exercise I learned from Lee Odell at the State University of New York at Albany, I ask people to form groups of three and to take turns reading aloud their own papers and responding to one another's reading:

A. To the reader: Read your paper out loud twice. After you have read, take notes according to the response you receive. Do not defend your piece of writing.

B. To the respondent: Listen carefully to each reader. After the second reading, respond orally in each of these two ways: (1) What struck you as interesting? (2) Where did you want more information?

More than any other workshop activity, this one places participants in the role of students, asking them to write on demand and then to submit that writing for evaluation. In this case, however, the evaluations are deliberately uncritical; the listener practices giving help without saying "good" or "bad." This exercise creates an anxiety-producing situation (reading *your* writing out loud) and then controls it by requiring participants to follow strict guidelines.

At the conclusion of this exercise, participants regroup and write briefly in their journals about how they felt writing and reading their writing. Finally, people share their observations, and we talk about the possible "lessons" for teachers who make writing assignments to students: (1) the value of writing for the generation of ideas (freewriting), (2) the importance of shaping freewriting toward an audience (revision), (3) the benefits of nonjudgmental peer response, (4) the difficulty (and excitement) of creating under pressure, and (5) the stimulation from having one's writing well received.

In two-day workshops participants revise their writing overnight, in the privacy of their quarters, and copy it onto ditto masters for duplication the following day. It is then possible to form larger writing groups, five or six each, and read and respond to a visible piece of writing. These groups meet for about two hours and set up their own response guidelines. This exercise allows participants to receive more precise suggestions for revision than did the oral reading the day before.

The second-day response groups reinforce for the participants the importance of feedback in the composing process, the necessity for incubation time to write well, the value of immediate, personal, oral response, and the embarrassment caused by even small misspellings. For many faculty members, especially those in scientific and technical fields, this is the first chance in years they have had to do a serious piece of personal writing; and while some may argue that the experience of such personal writing does not transfer to technical papers and laboratory reports, most recognize that the revision principles, broadly conceived, cut across disciplinary lines. Rewriting is rethinking, and rethinking makes learning possible.

This essay has argued that writing instructors who teach revision must teach their colleagues to teach it as well. Critical learning and communication skills do not develop in a vacuum, but rather from careful instruction and regular practice. Student writing will improve only when it becomes the concern of the entire university community; writing workshops that emphasize revision are one way for English teachers to share their concern.

Notes

1. James Britton, Tony Burgess, Nancy Martin, Alex McLeod, and Harold Rosen, *The Development of Writing Abilities (11–18),* Schools Council Research Studies (London: Macmillan Education, 1975).

2. Peter Elbow, *Writing without Teachers* (New York: Oxford University Press, 1973).

Psycholinguistic Perspectives on Revising

C. A. Daiute
Teachers College, Columbia University

Many teachers have hoped that modern linguistics would help solve the writing problems of their students. Indeed, both structural and transformational linguistics have been a successful part of the writing curriculum.[1] In recent years, however, writing teachers have questioned the wholesale application of the scientific study of grammar to the teaching of writing.[2] In many cases, abstract structural theories are not directly related to the activities of the writer. To understand writing behavior, we need to know about ongoing linguistic processes, such as how people produce spoken sentences and why they make mistakes. Psycholinguistics, the study of language use, is more likely to relate to the teaching of writing than is linguistics, the study of language structure.

Psycholinguistics includes the study of how cognitive processes such as memory and attention influence linguistic performance, and most psycholinguistic research has focused on sentence perception tasks like reading and listening.[3] Recently, however, psycholinguists have begun to study talking. My aim here is to show how psycholinguistic research on talking, and the related analysis of ungrammatical sentences, applies to writing, especially the writing of first drafts. Since talking and writing are both production processes, it is reasonable to consider their similarities.

Students in remedial writing classes do not have a monopoly on grammar mistakes. College professors, movie heroines, and highly paid newscasters also produce ungrammatical utterances, and listeners frequently do not notice the ungrammaticality. Consider these three examples.[4]

1. That's the first time anybody ever sang to me like that before.
2. I really enjoyed flying in an airplane that I understand how it works.

109

3. The recent outbreak of riots are disturbing to the peace efforts.

The first was uttered by Gloria Stewart to Dick Powell in the movie *Gold Diggers of 1935* after he had sung to her accompanied by a blaring radio. Since the meaning of the sentence is clear, most *Gold Diggers* fans did not notice the deviant grammatical structure. The second was made by a college professor who had just traveled in a propeller airplane, and the third by a newscaster.

Sentences like 1 and 2 illustrate a phenomenon that psycholinguists have examined for clues about how ideas are formed into sentences. Sentence 1 is a miscombining of two sentences. The initial sentence ("That's the first time anybody ever sang to me like that.") is overlapped and completed by a second sentence ("[Nobody] ever sang to me like that before."). The speaker began one sentence and finished another. In overlapping sentences, there is a medial sequence that can go with the initial and final sequences of the sentence separately. Here the overlapping sequence is "body ever sang to me like that." In sentence 2 the initial sequence is "I really enjoyed flying in an airplane that I understand." The overlapping sentence is "I understand how it works," and the medial sequence is "I understand."

Example 3 is a special case of phrase overlapping. The sequence "The recent outbreak of riots" overlaps "riots are disturbing to the peace efforts." As the phrases overlap, the modifier of the subject dominates the verb "are," which should agree with the singular head noun "outbreak." Such overlappings have been called "gobbled verb" sentences because the verb inflection is "gobbled" by an adjacent modifier.[5]

The errors in these three sentences are ones that English teachers recognize as frequent and sometimes persistent in writing. Most teachers do not, however, consider them to be evidence of a single process, and they are inclined to identify written syntax errors like those in the sentences below in a variety of ways: "awkward sentence," "subject/verb agreement error," "fragment."[6]

4. Four years ago was the best time of my career which I wasn't in a position to know that then.

5. This waste of two intelligent women I know would still be active if this boss never had such policies at work.

6. The classic beauty of the new Datsun models are a big seller this year.

7. By living in a dorm can be very noisy and distracting.

8. Society has set up certain limits of education which every citizen has to meet their standards.

9. The need for college in certain fields have drop[ped].

10. By limiting the open enrollment program won't help to solve the problem.

Researchers who study basic writing have noticed sentences with such structural problems but have not classified them as related. Mina Shaughnessy, from whose book sentences 8 and 9 were taken, explained them as typical errors illustrating different phenomena about writers' processes. Valerie Krishna, whose work contributed sentence 10, suggested that such serious written syntax problems defy analysis. When examined in the light of psycholinguistic analysis of speech errors, however, these structures seem less mysterious.[7] Figure 1 illustrates overlappings in these sentences.

Most prior studies of writing have emphasized the differences between speaking and writing.[8] Differences such as the form of expression and dependence on context are no doubt important, but it is also useful to understand how speaking and writing are influenced by the same cognitive capacities. The similarity of the structures in spoken and written errors illustrates how the initial stages of both oral and written sentence production are influenced by the same psychological processes and constraints.

Why do overlapping sentences occur? Psycholinguists argue that sentences like the ten examples above are the normal products of a language system constrained by short-term memory limits.[9] There is a limit to how much specific information we can hold in mind at one time; therefore, when a subject noun phrase is far from its modifier, we are likely to have trouble in combining the two.

Psychologists have found that the number of units that can be held in short-term memory is about seven.[10] Overlapping and gobbled sentences in writing have features that suggest they were caused by short-term memory limits. The error usually occurs more than seven words into the sentence and relatively far from the word with which it should be matched. For example, in sentence 6, the verb "are" is the ninth word in the sentence and is six words distant from the head noun "beauty." According to psycholinguistic explanation then, the head noun and all the other words before the verb burdened short-term memory; as a result, the writer forgot the original head noun and incorrectly based subject/verb agreement on the adjacent plural noun.

Linguistic structure, as well as number of words, interacts with short-term memory limits in a specific way during sentence perception and production. The clause is the basic unit that is stored exactly in short-term memory. The basic "perceptual clause" is a sequence including explicitly stated subject and predicate relations —a basic noun/verb pair.[11] After a perceptual clause is completed, it is erased from short-term memory and stored in long-term memory in semantic form. This process is called semantic recoding. After recoding, the listener or reader remembers the meaning of a clause but not its exact words. While completing a sentence, the speaker or writer continuously monitors the mean-

---

4. Four years ago was the best time of my career which I wasn't in a position to know that then.
   a. Four years ago was the best time of my career which <u>I wasn't in a position to know</u>
   b. <u>I wasn't in a position to know</u> that then

5. This waste of two intelligent women I know would still be active if this boss never had such policies at work.
   a. This waste of <u>two intelligent women I know</u>
   b. <u>two intelligent women I know</u> would still be active if this boss never had such policies at work

6. The classic beauty of the new Datsun models are a big seller this year.
   a. The classic beauty of <u>the new Datsun models</u>
   b. <u>the new Datsun models</u> are a big seller this year

7. By living in a dorm can be very noisy and distracting.
   a. By <u>living in a dorm</u>
   b. <u>living in a dorm</u> can be very noisy and distracting

8. Society has set up certain limits of education which every citizen has to meet their standards.
   a. Society has set up certain limits of education which <u>every citizen has to meet</u>
   b. <u>every citizen has to meet</u> their standards

9. The need for college in certain fields have drop[ped].
   a. The need for college <u>in certain fields have</u>
   b. <u>in certain fields have</u> drop[ped]

10. By limiting the open enrollment program won't help to solve the problem.
   a. By <u>limiting the open enrollment program</u>
   b. <u>limiting the open enrollment program</u> won't help to solve the problem

---

Figure 1. Overlapping sentences. Medial sequences are indicated by underlining.

ings of initial recoded clauses but does not remember specific grammatical markers such as phrase form, number, word order, or part of speech. For example, sentence 5 includes four potential perceptual clauses before the error:

    a. This waste of two intelligent women
    b. This waste of two intelligent women I know
    c. two intelligent women I know
    d. I know

During formation of this sentence, there were four points where the exact forms of initial clauses could have been erased and recoded into semantic form. Thus, recoding can account for why the writer based the predicate on "women" rather than on the structural head noun "waste," which, by hypothesis, had been forgotten.

As a preliminary test of the hypothesis that the limits of short-term memory account for syntax errors, I analyzed over a thousand sentences with syntax errors written by high-school seniors and college freshmen.[12] I found that overlapping and gobbled verb sentences as well as errors such as misplaced modifiers and nonparallel sentences have a mean number of eleven words and two perceptual clause boundaries before the sentence error is obvious. The presence of many words and several clause boundaries indicates that semantic recoding had occurred before the point of the error and that the initial part of the sentence had faded from short-term memory. Recoding of initial clauses makes syntactic features like phrase form, inflection, and placement inaccessible to writers as they add the final parts of sentences.

In summary, an overlapping sentence occurs when two parts of a sentence that depend on each other are separated by more than five words and appear in distinct perceptual clauses. After an initial perceptual clause is semantically recoded, grammatical details fade from the writer's memory. When composing a subsequent clause, the writer does not have access to important grammatical information. For example, when writing the verbs in sentences 6 and 9, the writers forgot whether the head nouns were singular or plural. While forming the final parts of sentences 7 and 10, the writers forgot the exact form of the initial phrases beginning with "by."

I have demonstrated that analyses of syntax errors in speech can apply to at least two frequently occurring classes of syntax errors in writing. This relationship suggests that psycholinguistics will be useful in the study of writing. This analysis also suggests that the process of writing sentences—at least in first drafts—is like the process of talking. Writers of course have more chance than speakers to correct awkward sentences, and experienced writers usually recognize and repair syntax errors even as they quickly write first drafts. On the other hand, beginning writers may tend to behave like speakers. They tend to write down speech, their familiar productive mode. Moreover, merely rereading sentences may not help because similar memory limits hold for perception as for production of clauses.

The psycholinguistic study of sentences with syntax errors suggests, as other studies have before, that writers should be encouraged to compose freely, unencumbered by concerns about "grammar," punctuation, spelling. In the light of psycholinguistic study, one can see that producing correct sentences is difficult because of such natural processes as semantic recoding. Planning, forming, evaluating, and revising sentences in one step burden short-term memory, which constrains even the basic speaking process. It is difficult enough to make sure that *all* the ideas and words of a first draft are the right ones. Struggling against semantic recoding in order to hold grammatical details as well as the meaning of prior clauses in short-term memory is bound to hamper further the writer's composing process.

During composing, writers should be free to generate, discover, and explore ideas; they must then also translate them into clauses and sentences. Peter Elbow expresses the dilemma for students trying to write perfect drafts all at once.

> Editing *in itself* is not the problem. Editing is usually necessary if we want to end up with something satisfactory. The problem is that editing goes on *at the same time* as producing. The editor, as it were, is constantly looking over the shoulder of the producer fiddling with what he's doing while he's in the middle of trying to do it. No wonder the producer gets nervous, jumpy, inhibited, and finally can't be coherent. It's an unnecessary burden to try to think of words and also worry at the same time whether they're the right words.[13]

The psycholinguistic study of errors also suggests that writers may need to use explicit sentence analysis strategies when revising in order to identify errors that are influenced by processes also occurring during reading. Since the limits of short-term memory hold during perception as well as during production, merely rereading sentences may not help beginning writers. Sentence analysis, however, helps writers break their sentences down into the most important structural units like the basic subject, verb, and object. Writers can then hold reduced sentence schemas in mind while evaluating the coherence of the overall structures. Such analyses need not be complex nor rely on linguistic terminology.

Beginning writers may have more trouble holding linguistic structures in mind because they are not familiar with the variety of common written sentence forms. Experienced writers have developed strategies to use during revision and they are familiar with a variety of complex linguistic structures. For example, when beginning a sentence with "by," experienced writers remember that they are forming a subordinate unit that will eventually have to be added to an independent clause.

Another reason why explicit training in sentence analysis may be necessary is that perceptual completeness is not the same as grammatical completeness. Writers must identify the grammatically complete units that are required in written English. For example, the sentence fragment "Because computers are nothing compared to playing" is a complete perceptual clause but is not a complete sentence. A writer may punctuate such a clause as a complete sentence because the perceptual system has identified it as complete, has erased it from short-term memory, and has stored only the meaning. Thus, writers need strategies for evaluating sentence completeness. As writers become familiar with many structures, they can build up sets of sentence frames and use markers like initial prepositions or subordinating conjunctions as signals that specific sentence patterns will be required in later parts of the sentence. Such automatic sentence pattern frames condense the information to be held in short-term memory and thus reduce some of the burden on it.

A successful heuristic for sentence analysis can be based on sector analysis,[14] which involves sentence evaluation procedures that help students to identify easily major sentence parts and the relationships among them. For example, turning sentences into questions that can be answered by "yes" or "no" often helps students to identify sentence subjects.

Sector analysis is a major part of two evaluation procedures— telegramming and sentence *un*combining—and I have used both to help students evaluate the grammatical coherence of their sentences. I ask students who have trouble revising gobbled verb sentences to reduce them to telegrams. They do this by underlining the three or four most important words in the sentence. This act helps them realize that the first words of the sentence—

the words that they had originally intended as the subject—are no longer grammatically connected to the sentence. The students then uncombine the gobbled verb sentence and find that the second part of it is a complete and independent sentence. If the writer intended to write about the initial head noun, he or she now has an opportunity to add an appropriate predicate. Figure 2 illustrates how students can use this procedure.

Example of a Sentence with a Gobbled Verb

The classic beauty of the new Datsun models are a big seller this year.

Correction Procedure

1. Identify the complete subject by turning the sentence into a yes/no question. (are The classic beauty of the new Datsun models ~~are~~ a big seller this year?) At this point, students often notice that the verb is incorrect because it is now adjacent to its subject.

2. Mark an X over the word you moved to make the question and an X over the position from which you moved the word. (aͯre The classic beauty of the new Datsun models aͯ~~re~~ a big seller this year?)

3. The words between the Xs make up the subject. Draw a box around the subject. (aͯre │The classic beauty of the new Datsun models│ aͯ~~re~~ a big seller this year?)

4. Underline the three most important words, one in the subject, one in the verb, and one in the rest of the sentence. (The classic <u>beauty</u> of the new Datsun models <u>are</u> a big <u>seller</u> this year.)

5. Circle the verb and the word in the subject it agrees with. (The classic <u>beauty</u> of the new Datsun (models) (are) a big <u>seller</u> this year.)

6. Draw an arrow from the verb to the word it should agree with. (The classic <u>beauty</u> of the new Datsun (models) (are) a big <u>seller</u> this year.)

7. Correct the sentence. If the verb is wrong, correct it. If you forgot to make a statement about the word you originally intended to write about, complete the sentence. (For example: The classic beauty of the new Datsun models is a big seller this year. The new Datsun models are a big seller this year. The classic beauty of the new Datsun models attracts buyers.)

Figure 2. Correcting a sentence with a gobbled verb. From "Overlapping and Gobbled Sentences: Insights from Psycholinguistics," a paper delivered by C. A. Daiute at the convention of the National Council of Teachers of English, 1978.

When students are unable to recognize problems in specific overlapping sentences, I ask them to uncombine them into two or three sentences. After writing the shorter sentences, students describe the relationship between them. They then recombine the clauses by selecting from a list of relative pronouns, coordinating conjunctions, and subordinating conjunctions. Students who continue to miscombine the same sentence are guided through further, gradually developing exercises for repairing overlapping sentences.

Telegramming and sentence uncombining give students shorthand structural maps of their ungrammatical and awkward sentences, thus enabling them to hold all the key parts of a sentence in mind at once to check for overall coherence. Telegramming and uncombining also presumably build up their repertoires of typical English grammatical structures and the ways in which they can be reduced and expanded. Interestingly, the limits of short-term memory may also suggest one reason why sentence-combining exercises have been so successful—combining exercises that build incrementally by expanding basic structures teach the basic sentence forms and may increase the writer's memory for such forms. *Un*combining and recombining anomalous structures may repeat and reinforce this process. Reducing combined structures may be necessary if the lengths of resulting sentences in sentence combining exercises overburden the writer's short-term memory.

Although writing and speaking differ in various important ways, the similarity of oral and written sentence errors supports the view that the early steps in writing are similar to those in talking. They share the same underlying cognitive factors influencing the transformation of ideas into sentences. The suggestion that writers are constrained in much the same way as speakers can help teachers see writing errors as indicators of processes and constraints underlying the performance of their students. Understanding these processes can help teachers devise sentence revision exercises that build incrementally on ones that do not tax the relative short-term memory capacities of their students. Analysis exercises can also help students develop automatic sentence pattern frames to use as aids in remembering sentences while they evaluate them. This study of oral and written sentence errors suggests that experimental and theoretical data gleaned from the study of language can be applied usefully to the classroom, but this application is at its best when it is based on a theory of language use.

Notes

1. The application of transformational grammar to the teaching of writing is discussed in Donald R. Bateman and Frank J. Zidonis, *The Effect of a Study of Transformational Grammar on the Writing of Ninth and Tenth Graders* (Urbana, Ill.: National Council of Teachers of English, 1966); in Elaine Chaika, "Grammars and Teaching," *College English* 39 (March 1978): 770-83; and in John C. Mellon, *Transformational Sentence Combining: A Method for Enhancing the Development of Syntactic Fluency in English Composition* (Urbana, Ill.: National Council of Teachers of English, 1969). The application of structural grammar is discussed in Robert L. Allen, *English Grammars and English Grammar* (New York: Charles Scribner's Sons, 1974); in R. L. Allen, R. L. Pompian, and D. A. Allen, *Working Sentences* (New York: Thomas Y. Crowell Co., 1975); in Louis T. Milic, "Composition via Stylistics," in *Linguistics, Stylistics, and the Teaching of Composition,* ed. Donald McQuade (Akron, Ohio: University of Akron, 1979), pp. 91-102; in Mildred Rothman, Sheila Pyros, Irene Hyman, Colette Daiute, and Barry Karp, "Educational Skills: A Global Approach," *Insight* (1976): 15-18 (published by State University of New York at Albany); and in Hortense A. Sarot, Responses to William J. Linn, *College English* 38 (March 1977): 731-34 and 39 (October 1977): 241-42.

2. Gary Tate, "The Open Mind: Linguistics and the Writer," in *Teaching High School Composition,* eds. Gary Tate and Edward P. J. Corbett (New York: Oxford University Press, 1970), p. 159.

3. Major psycholinguistic research is reviewed in J. A. Fodor, T. G. Bever, and M. F. Garrett, *The Psychology of Language* (New York: McGraw-Hill, 1974); in H. H. Clark and E. V. Clark, *Psychology and Language: An Introduction to Psycholinguistics* (New York: Harcourt Brace Jovanovich, 1977); and in Dan I. Slobin, *Psycholinguistics,* 2d ed. (Glenview, Ill.: Scott Foresman and Co., 1979).

4. The first two examples appear in T. G. Bever, J. M. Carroll, and R. Hurtig, "Analogy or Ungrammatical Sequences That Are Utterable and Comprehensible Are the Origins of New Grammars in Language Acquisition and Linguistic Evolution," in *An Integrated Theory of Linguistic Ability,* eds. T. G. Bever, J. J. Katz, and D. T. Langendoen (New York: Thomas Y. Crowell Co., 1976), p. 149 and p. 150 respectively. The third was cited by C. A. Daiute, "Structural Similarities between Writing and Talking" (Paper given at the Conference on College Composition and Communication, 1980).

5. I have borrowed the term *gobbled* from John M. Carroll, "The Perceptual Principle of 'Gobbling': A Study in Functional Linguistic Explanation" (Paper given at the Northeast Linguistic Society Conference, University of Montreal, 1975).

6. Sentence (4) appears in C. A. Daiute, "Overlapping and Gobbled Sentences: Insights from Psycholinguistics" (Paper presented at the convention of the National Council of Teachers of English, 1978). Sentence (5) is found in C. A. Daiute, "A Psycholinguistic Study of Writing" (Ph. D. diss., Teachers College, Columbia University, 1980), p. 69. Sentences (6) and (7) come from Daiute, "Overlapping and Gobbled Sen-

tences." Sentences (8) and (9) were cited by Mina P. Shaughnessy, *Errors and Expectations: A Guide for the Teacher of Basic Writing* (New York: Oxford University Press, 1977), p. 64 and p. 116 respectively. Sentence (10) appears in Valerie Krishna, "The Syntax of Error," *Basic Writing: Error 1* (Spring 1975): 43.

7. Overlapping sentences like (4), (2), and (8) appear simply to include substituted conjunctions. One could suspect that the speaker of (2) intended to use "when" rather than "that." Similarly, people have suggested to me that the writers of (4) and (8) might have intended to use "but" or "so." One can distinguish between misused conjunctions and overlapping sentences in several ways. First, one can ask the speaker or writer what he or she intended. The speaker of (2) explained that he did not intend to use "when" to express a temporal relation between the clauses. He intended to modify "airplane" by using a structure such as "an airplane the workings of which I understand."

If a student frequently writes overlapping sentences including relative pronouns that seem to be intended as conjunctions, one can test the student's knowledge of the uses of particular relative pronouns by examining his or her writing. "Fill-in" and "sentence-completion" exercises also show whether or not a student can use a relative pronoun as a conjunction. It is also possible that an overlapping sentence results because the speaker or writer begins a sentence in a form that can be completed correctly *only* by a structure that he or she has never before used. The ungrammatical sentence could be an avoidance of an unfamiliar structure. Even if this is the case, the fact that the option is an overlapping sentence supports the feasibility of this phenomenon.

One reason why such sentences take the form they do and why they are produced by all types of speakers and writers may be that if local sequences are acceptable, the ungrammaticality or awkwardness of larger structures may be overlooked. The limits of short-term memory influence this process as initial sequences that set the overall syntactic structure of a sentence fade from memory.

8. Discussion of important differences between speaking and writing appear in Janet Emig, "Writing as a Mode of Learning," *College Composition and Communication* 28 (May 1977): 122-28; and in Barry M. Kroll, "Cognitive Egocentrism and the Problem of Audience Awareness in Written Discourse," *Research in the Teaching of English* 12 (October 1978): 269-81.

9. Bever, Carroll, and Hurtig, "Analogy or Ungrammatical Sequences"; and Daiute, "A Psycholinguistic Study of Writing."

10. George Miller, "The Magical Number Seven, Plus or Minus Two: Some Limits on Our Capacity for Processing Information," *Psychological Review* 63 (1956): 81-97.

11. Discussion of the role of perceptual (functional) clauses as recoding units appears in J. M. Carroll, "The Interaction of Structural and Functional Variables in Sentence Perception: Some Preliminary Studies" (Ph. D. diss., Columbia University, 1976); in J. M. Carroll and T. G. Bever, "Sentence Comprehension: A Study in the Relation of Knowledge to Perception," in *The Handbook of Perception: Speech and Language,* eds. E. C. Carterette and M. P. Friedman (New York: Academic Press,

1976); in J. M. Carroll and M. Tanenhaus, "Functional Clauses and Sentence Segmentation," *Journal of Speech and Hearing Research* 21, no. 4 (1978): 793–808; and in J. M. Carroll, "Functional Completeness as a Determinant of Processing Load during Sentence Comprehension," *Language and Speech* 22 (1979): 347–69.

12. Daiute, "A Psycholinguistic Study of Writing." I am further studying the relationship between the short-term memory capacities of sixth- through twelfth-grade writers and the syntax errors in their writing. This research is funded by the National Institute of Education.

13. Peter Elbow, *Writing without Teachers* (London: Oxford University Press, 1973), p. 5.

14. Allen, Pompian, and Allen, *Working Sentences.*

The Cloze Test
as a Diagnostic Tool for Revision

Ken Davis
University of Kentucky

The cloze test, developed in the 1950s by Wilson L. Taylor, presents a passage of prose in which certain words have been deleted and asks the reader to "guess" what the missing words are.[1] The number of correct guesses can be used to measure the comprehension skill of the reader and the comprehensibility of the passage. I suggest that composition teachers take advantage of the latter measurement potential by asking student to run cloze tests on their rough drafts as a means of identifying areas in need of revision.

For the past year my students have used this technique in freshman and advanced composition classes and in business-writing workshops at a local industrial plant. Each student prepares a cloze test by counting back a hundred words or so from the end of his or her draft and underlining every nth word in that passage. (N can be as small as five; ten is a handy number that provides slightly more context.) The student then recopies this hundred-word passage, substituting numbered blanks of uniform length for the underlined words, folds under the original passage in the rough draft, and gives both sheets of paper to a classmate. The fellow student reads the draft down to the fold, skips to the version with the blanks, and lists his or her guesses for the missing words on a separate sheet of paper. After three such readings, all guesses are returned to the writer for analysis.

To facilitate this analysis, I distribute the following form:

Blank #	Your word	Reader 1	Reader 2	Reader 3	H or M	+ or −
1						
2						

Students insert the deleted word for each blank along with the guesses of the three readers. If at least two of the readers guessed correctly, an *H* for "hit" is recorded in the next column; otherwise, an *M* for "miss" is inserted.

At this point I explain why we have done all this. As readers read (I tell my students), they make subconscious predictions about upcoming words. If these expectations are usually fulfilled, the reading comes easily; if not, the passage is difficult and seems to lack a certain "flow." Readers, then, are always making hits and misses; I illustrate the varieties of hits and misses with this simple diagram:

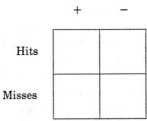

Most hits, I suggest, are positive: that is, they signal positive features in the student's draft. The student who wrote the example below got three correct guesses of "they"; this "hit" attests to a useful anaphoric relationship she has set up between the subjects of the two clauses.

1. People who live in the past lose the present because _____ are unable to. . .

Negative hits, however, are certainly possible. As critics, whether of novels or student themes, we often use "predictable" as a pejorative term, suggesting that writing that never surprises is as bad as writing that always does. Yet in administering cloze tests on hundreds of student drafts, I have found only a handful of hits that I am willing to call "negative." Most occur in trite phrases:

2. You can't please _____ of the people all of the time.

Most student writers in my experience, however, err on the side of *un*predictability, at least at the stylistic level measured by the cloze test. Perhaps the "predictability" we hope to find in student papers occurs at "higher," more conceptual levels.

So to the "misses," much more useful than the hits as diagnostic tools. Most misses, I suggest, are negative, pinpointing unfulfilled reader expectations that can be better fulfilled through revision. Some simply signal shifts in person:

3. I discovered that _____ must . . .

Here, the unanimous guess of "I" convinced the writer that his word "one" was a bad choice. The student who wrote this example made a similar discovery:

4. The majority of voters can't participate because candidates won't let them. This will continue to alienate _____ until politicians show . . .

She learned from the guesses of "voters" and "people" that her word "us" shifted the established subject from third to first person.

But the cloze test can also reveal more elusive anaphoric weaknesses. A student discussing the women's movement described at some length the stereotypical feminist and then began a second description:

5. To the opposite extreme of the liberated _____ there is the completely submissive woman.

His word "progressive" had not been used before in the paper and therefore did not serve as an effective link with the first description. All readers guessed "woman," and most later agreed that it would have clarified the otherwise good attempt at transition. Another writer, after reporting on the seriousness of the present energy crisis, began her conclusion as follows:

6. The crisis will be _____ worse in years to come, so we need to . . .

Most readers guessed "even," thus providing a more skillful transition from the body of the paper than the writer's word, "much."

Other transition problems are also revealed:

7. The format was a success, _____ mainly because of the answers revealed by the surveys.

The writer of this example had "but" in the blank; when readers guessed "and," he was able to profit from a class discussion of Winterowd's "grammar of coherence" and the relationships signaled by various connective words.

Besides relationship problems, the cloze test also pinpoints weaknesses in diction:

8. America's economic situation is partly caused by people still believing in the myth of unlimited natural resources that we have had in the past instead of facing the reality of the present shortages. These _____ show how we must focus on the present if we wish to remain in control of ourselves.

This student had written "things"; her readers guessed "shortages," "problems," and "examples"—all more precise terms. Here are other passages from student drafts; in each, the writer's word is placed in the blank, the readers' guesses in brackets after it:

9. Carol didn't think much about the comment at the time, but later in the evening she was [became] really concerned.

10. A warm glow is felt by those who completed [accepted, survived] the challenge of Sky-Bridge.

11. Nobody can steal the past; it is ours to cherish [keep] for the rest of our lives.

12. Their lives are more together and organized [productive, happy].

The writer of example 9 was able to see from the guesses that her verb, "was," belied the actual process of *becoming* concerned that Carol probably experienced. Classmates pointed out to the author of 10 that challenges can be "accepted" or even "survived," but not really "completed." In 11, "cherish" is imprecise as a contrast to "steal." And the writer of 12 began to go wrong not at the obliterated word but two words earlier: the imprecision of "together" makes further prediction difficult, and, in any case, "organized" seems redundant.

Occasionally the cloze test signals a particular diction problem, the failure to provide idiomatic co-occurrence:

13. . . . believing that man is the boss and that woman is a servant complying to [with] all of his commands and desires.

And many misses result from "global" failures—overall imprecision and general lack of substance in a passage:

14. People look at other people today and see the happiness [differences, good, faults] in them. Many times the past [consequence, result] is sad and people punish themselves [unjustly,

them]. Only the unhappy want to <u>bring</u> [build, dig] up the bad a person <u>experienced</u> [was, committed, had] in the past.

Finally, to complete the four-cell matrix, I discuss the "positive" misses, almost as rare in student drafts as the negative hits:

15. These people are also unable to accept new ideas and concepts because they refuse to give up <u>tradition</u> [things].
16. I also like to sit and watch the squirrels collect nuts for the winter, or listen to the singing of a <u>bluejay</u> [bird] in the spring.

These sentences, the opposite of example 8, show writers using a more precise word than was predicted by readers and thus providing an informative surprise. I gave sentence 16 to an entire class for guessing; when I revealed the missing word as "bluejay" after all had guessed "bird," the pleasure of the students was audible. From then on, we adopted the term "bluejay" as a codeword for positive misses of this kind, and I began to see students trying to incorporate more bluejays into their writing.

As a last step in the cloze test, students code each of their hits and misses as "+" or "–" and then discuss specific examples as a group. Finally, they return to their drafts, looking for ways to increase the number of positive hits and misses. Sometimes, of course, they are able to turn misses into hits simply by substituting the guessed word for the original, but more often they begin to look at the context that caused the unfulfilled prediction to be made.

At least four reasons, I suggest, make the cloze test an effective diagnostic tool for revision. First, it brings an awareness of reader needs directly into the composing process. Far too much instruction in writing is centered on the product rather than on the reader, and we sometimes forget that writing is important *only* as something to be read. Students who conduct cloze tests of their rough drafts confront directly the needs of their audience.

Second, the empirical, even quantitative, nature of the cloze test gives students "hard" data on the readability of their writing. Students often regard a teacher's reaction to their writing as subjective and idiosyncratic; the same reaction revealed by a cloze test seems more objective, less whimsical. And although I urge students to draw no inferences from their overall "hit" score on such a small sample, the results have a scientific feel that many students welcome.

Third, the cloze test brings a certain precision to the revision process, focusing as it does on specific words and their relation to the larger context. It's one thing to tell a student that a paragraph doesn't "flow"; it's quite another and vastly more helpful thing to say, "Here and here and here you fail to fulfill the expectations you created there and there and there."

Fourth, the cloze test capitalizes on the inherent efficiency of "sampling." By its focus on a small number of randomly selected words, it provides for more detailed attention than could be given to a whole paper. After areas for revisions are identified in this small sample, students can begin to attack them throughout their work.

Clearly, work can be done to make the cloze test an even more effective tool for revision. The relationship between cloze score and overall quality of the writing, measured independently, can be explored further. And my four-cell matrix, or some variation on it, can perhaps be expanded into a more detailed heuristic for student analysis of cloze test results, for example, categorizing misses as syntactic or semantic.

But even in my yet unsophisticated use of the cloze test, I have found it a powerful tool for helping students identify areas for revision in their writing. Frank Smith notes that "it may be from the perspective of predictions and intentions that one can best perceive the intimate relationship between readers and writers. It might be said that a book is comprehended (from the writer's point of view at least) when the reader's predictions mirror the writer's intentions."[2] The cloze test works as a revision technique because it checks for this mirroring in time to do the writer some good.

Notes

1. Wilson L. Taylor, "Applications of Cloze and Entropy Measures to the Study of Contextual Constraints in Samples of Continuous Prose" (Ph. D. diss., University of Illinois, 1954), *Dissertation Abstracts* 15 (1955): 464-65.

2. Frank Smith, *Understanding Reading: A Psycholinguistic Analysis of Reading and Learning to Read,* 2d ed. (New York: Holt, Rinehart and Winston, 1978), p. 171.

On Parapraxes and Revision

Robert Gregory
Carnegie-Mellon University

"Successful revision is, after all, a re-vision, a new and clearer view."[1] "Style is outlook and . . . outlook is discovered through the act of writing itself."[2] These statements represent a common and useful viewpoint on revision, that is, that the first draft is a *fully conscious* but rhetorically ineffective product. This is true to a great extent, but when we read over our own work or the work of others, we also realize that *unconscious* material is present as well, most visibly in the form of one type of the Freudian parapraxes, the slip of the pen. My purpose here is to suggest that paying attention to these slips can be a fruitful form of revision in two particular cases, that of the inexperienced writer alienated from topic or approach without being aware of it, and that of the experienced writer who finds his or her work satisfactory but somehow not quite genuine. I don't at all recommend immediate psychoanalysis in such cases; rather, I suggest writers will find it useful to follow Freud's idea that these slips have a sense of their own:

> What do we mean by "has a sense"? That the product of the slip of the tongue may perhaps itself have a right to be regarded as a completely valid psychical act, pursuing an aim of its own, as a statement with a content and significance. So far we have always spoken of parapraxes but it seems now as though sometimes the faulty act was itself quite a *normal* act, which merely took the place of the other act which was the one expected or intended.[3]

In other words, the slip is not the appearance of abnormality but the collision of two normal expressions, one consciously intended and one unconsciously intended.

This concept can be usefully applied to the most immediate problem in teaching inexperienced writers to revise. It's not that they don't know how, but that they don't want to. Their position

127

is that revision is a Platonic ideal that contradicts the traditional wisdom of humanity—a bird in the hand (turkey or not) is better than two in the bush. They can be shown that revised papers earn better grades than first drafts, of course, but it is even more persuasive to show them that the first draft may be a message from a foreign country, which, on the one hand, it might be embarrassing to make public and which, on the other and better, can when decoded yield a more genuine topic or a more genuine approach to a topic. And as is well known, the generating principle of good writing is the energy-supplying assurance that what is being expressed is genuine and therefore important.

Although we are all familiar with slips of the pen, consider for a moment several examples.

1. In a generally spiritless classification analysis of his ethnic group, the writer decided that close family ties were an identifying factor. He called one cause of that closeness strict discipline, which was an important factor, he went on to say, in causing families to "sick together."

2. In a bland cause-effect analysis of apathy toward reading on the part of high-school students, a Hispanic writer mentioned that those who did not read would not go to college and would thus be stuck "in a life of manuel labor."

3. In an assignment to classify food as either health food or junk food, a student introduced the topic this way: "Health foods are considered to be any junk food that contain insufficient nutritional values." "Non" was penciled in before "junk" but "insufficient" was let stand.

4. In an essay on classes of music, the writer made an angry remark about minstrel shows as degrading to blacks, but in general wrote insipidly about black culture and its music. However, his thesis was expressed this way: "Throughout history, music has been apart of black culture."

In all of these cases, it could be objected that the slips are not genuine parapraxes. But all mistakes are parapraxes (even "the the") when we see that they are caused by lack of attention. The real question is this: which slips can be interpreted? I treated these as if they could be, using the general evidence of boredom or superficiality in the papers in question as an indication that the writers were of two minds and that those two minds had interfered with each other. With regard to example one, the writer in question colored when he had the slip pointed out. Writer number two was at first embarrassed and then delighted with the bitter tang of his pun "manuel/manual," a pun that accurately reflects the status quo in California. Writer three quite readily admitted that the slip reflected his genuine position that the distinction between health food and junk food was absurd. Writer four was baffled by the meaning of his slip and insisted that he thought of black music as part of his culture, not apart from it. In each case, however, the writer, whether he acknowledged parapraxis or not, was convinced that his first draft contained material that he should carefully observe and decode—and that, I think, inculcated an interest in revision more effectively than indicating rhetorical errors would have done. Suggesting a bad alignment between writer, topic, and approach certainly takes priority over pointing out less fundamental rhetorical inadequacies. My experience may not hold true for everyone, but I think those who teach beginners will agree that examples of unintended humor or unintended contradiction are not uncommon. If these slips are pointed out in private (and without mockery, of course) and are followed up in class by a brief discussion of Freudian slips, I believe parapraxes can be useful in stimulating the revision process.

Nor do I think such slips are found only in the writing of beginners, nor are they of use only to beginners. Consider Leon Edel's discussion of the early Henry James novel, *Watch and Ward:*

> Both the serial and book versions—published eight years apart—contain a passage in which Roger wonders after adopting Nora whether at the worst a little precursory love-making would do any harm. "The ground might be gently tickled to receive his own sowing; the petals of a young girl's nature, playfully forced apart, would leave the golden heart of a flower but the more accessible to his own vertical rays." This is a curious passage to come from an inveterate reader of French novels. It may have been penned tongue-in-cheek; yet it also represents a certain unconscious eroticism. Another and better-known passage in the novel describes Nora, in deshabille at bedtime, bringing her watch to be wound, with Roger's key proving a "misfit" and Hubert Lawrence's rather more successful even though "some rather intimate fumbling was needed to adjust it to Nora's diminutive timepiece." These passages survived the close revision of *Watch and Ward* in 1878. . . .[4]

Or consider the following, cited by Freud, from the casket scene in *Merchant of Venice;* Portia is speaking:

> . . . I could teach you
> How to choose right, but then I am forsworn;
> So will I never be; so may you miss me;
> But if you do, you'll make me wish a sin,
> That I have been forsworn. Beshrew your eyes,
> They have o'erlooked me and divided me;
> One half of me is yours, *the other half yours—*
> *Mine own, I would say* . . . [italics mine]. (act 3, scene 2)

If, on the one hand, Henry James can make such slips, and if, on the other, Shakespeare, as Freud points out, can have his characters make them for artistic effect,[5] then experienced writers may find something useful here. Whereas a student-writer may be used to repressing his or her genuine attitude in order to "get it over with," an experienced writer tries not to fall into such a situation. However, I would suggest that when one has finished a piece of work that seems perfectly all right and yet somehow all wrong, parapraxes should be searched for; the revision problem in this case is that the work seems closed and invulnerable, so that finding a slip can open it up again for further work.

The search in this case should begin with an examination of the figures of speech. For example, Washington Irving in his essay on the "Royal Poet" tends to contradict his ostensible thesis:

> As an amatory poem, it is edifying in these days of coarser thinking to notice the Nature, refinement, and exquisite delicacy which pervade it, banishing every gross thought or immodest expression and presenting female loveliness *clothed* in all its chivalrous attributes of almost supernatural purity and grace [my italics].[6]

Here Irving approves chaste depiction and at the same time imagines a naked female; we may have either an irruption of the unconscious or an example of what Kenneth Burke sees as the peculiar operation of the negative in language: ". . . whereas an injunction such as 'thou shalt not kill' is understandable enough as a negative *idea,* it also has about its edges the positive *image* of killing."[7] Whichever, tropes are sometimes unwitting contradictions of the offered idea, and examination of them may allow a writer a way back into a paper that needs work but seems finished at the same time. After all, if Prospero, that master of control, finds in the representation of the masque that he is projecting from his mind an image of repressed passion and anger in the dance of the sickle men (intending to celebrate the joys of lawful fecundity but hiding a wish to kill the monster in himself),[8] then we lesser magicians should look to our masques as well.

Notes

1. Sylvan Barnet and Marcia Stubbs, *Barnet and Stubbs's Practical Guide to Writing,* rev. ed. (Boston: Little, Brown and Co., 1977), p. 23.

2. Richard M. Eastman, *Style: Writing and Reading as the Discovery of Outlook,* 2d. ed. (New York: Oxford University Press, 1978), p. ix.

3. Sigmund Freud, *Introductory Lectures on Psychoanalysis,* trans. James Strachey (New York: W. W. Norton and Co., 1966), p. 35.

4. Leon Edel, *Henry James: The Conquest of London, 1870-1881* (New York: Avon Books, 1978), pp. 44-45.

5. Freud, p. 38.

6. Washing Irving, *The Sketchbook* (New York: New American Library, Signet Books, 1961), pp. 94-95. [Editor's note: This author error has been preserved from the original manuscript as an illustration of parapraxis. Washing Irving, indeed! Washing away those coarse thoughts, no doubt.]

7. Kenneth Burke, *Language as Symbolic Action: Essays on Life, Literature, and Method* (Berkeley: University of California, 1966), p. 10.

8. *The Tempest,* act 4, scene 1.

Revision and Improvement: Making the Connection

Gayle L. Smith
The Pennsylvania State University, Worthington Scranton
Campus

When I teach composition, I give students the opportunity to rewrite or revise graded papers for reevaluation. The few who decide that topics themselves were the source of their difficulty may or may not write greatly improved papers, but they do write papers that clearly demand new consideration. For the larger number of students who elect to work with the same basic idea and revise their first drafts, the situation is often more difficult. Despite my distinction between revising and editing, my warning about putting the first version out of sight and out of mind while revising, too many students do little more than edit and recopy their original papers.

Two main obstacles seem to prevent students from revising in the ways we have in mind when we urge them to do so. As writers and readers, particularly as experienced readers of student compositions, we are very aware of the endless possibilities and choices inherent in any writing task. I must have read forty narratives about the first day of deer season in the past three years, but no two shared much more than that basic topic. Oddly enough, student writers often are not fully aware of the fact that they have made choices; they feel that the way they wrote was rather inevitable. Revising then becomes a painful if not impossible task. They are attached to their words with a tenacity that is surprising. I discovered the extent to which this is true quite by accident when I asked my students to complete a sentence-combining exercise in class, turn in the papers, and work with the same exercise again for homework. Despite the fact that I urged them to take more time and to feel free to add details and rearrange the original order of the sentences, even without their first drafts available to them, many students produced paragraphs almost identical to those they had written in class. Even when our students are ready and willing to approach their subjects anew, they often do not seem to recognize what demands attention in their papers. When we advise them to write clear topic sentences, to concentrate on conveying an interesting impression, to use vivid sensory details, we know what we mean in terms of dozens of successful examples. To us these are sensible descriptions of what successful writers do; to our students they are apt to be abstract prescriptions which they nevertheless attempt to follow, sometimes surprising and even dismaying us.

Fortunately, some students do revise their work successfully, moving closer and closer to the basic objectives of the assignment at hand. Taking as my text one such three-draft effort, I developed an exercise that addresses the nature and objectives of revision and also reveals a good deal about how students understand and misunderstand our prescriptions for good writing. The apparent simplicity of the assignment addressed by the sample papers (describing a place, the first major assignment in a developmental writing course) made it an ideal text for us. Students were aware of the demands of this assignment almost from the beginning of the composition courses in which I used the exercise, and it was best to discuss revision early in the term. More important, here the larger matters such as the presence of a controlling idea, the organization, and the use of vivid and appropriate details stood out more dramatically than they might have in a paper with more sophisticated rhetorical purposes. In order to avoid further confusing the processes of revising and editing, I corrected distracting grammatical and mechanical errors in the three versions before distributing them. Additionally, I wanted to demonstrate to students that papers without such errors still may not be good papers.

Since I wanted students to test their understanding of the objectives for this assignment (or, perhaps more pragmatically, to test their understanding of my understanding), I distributed the three versions—each version reproduced on paper of a different color—without indicating the order in which they had been written. (A coding system other than color might, of course, be used.) Instead, I told students that I had found each paper an improvement over its predecessor and that both the writer and I had been quite satisfied with the third version; then I asked them to determine the order in which the papers had been written. The three papers, not necessarily in the order in which they were composed, appear below.[1] Keeping in mind that they were written early in a

developmental course in an effort to describe a place with clear
sensory details that supported a controlling impression, can you
discern a clear progression?

My Bedroom [blue version]

My bedroom is a very plain and simple room. Its light
blue walls are partially covered with posters of well known
people such as O. J. Simpson and Rocky. In the corner is my
desk. This desk is covered with little tokens which have
added up over the years. One of these tokens is a trophy
which I won in 1972 when our biddy basketball team won
the championship. Another memory piece is a varsity letter
which I received for playing baseball as a junior. Over on
the other side of the room is a light brown dresser which
makes a good stand for my tape player. The tape player, with
all kinds of tapes piled on top of it and on top of its speakers,
makes it difficult to see the mirror which is directly behind
it. On the mirror are stickers which I put on there when I was
young. These stickers sport the names of my favorite baseball and football teams such as the Phillies and Eagles.
Hanging from the side of the mirror is a baseball hat which
has the emblem of the New York Mets on the front. This hat
has been there for as long as I can remember. Besides being
the room of a typical teenager, I feel that this room holds
many memories which will not be forgotten for a long time.

The Bedroom [yellow version]

As we stand in the doorway, we can hear a sort of hum-
ming sound coming out of the room. As we enter the room,
we realize that my tape player has been left on without a
tape in it. As we add some light to the situation, we can see
that the tape player is covered with all kinds of little tokens
such as trophies, ash trays, and tapes. It sort of looks like a
junk yard for all the things that cannot be put anywhere
else. Above my tape player are three shelves which have
books stacked one on top of another in every which way.
These books are a storage place for all of the old papers that
I used in high school. On one of the shelves is a lamp with a
shade which has turned yellow with age. The switch for this
lamp is broken and the bulb has to be turned to make it go
on. On one wall are a couple of posters with faces of people
like O. J. Simpson and Rocky appearing on them. The posters
are curled at the bottom because the scotch tape fell off. All
over the floor are dirty clothes which need to be washed. It
looks as if this room is a giant hamper. This room looks as
if it is a storage room for junk of all kinds. In the middle of
the ceiling is a round light surrounded by a decorative chrome
piece. The ceiling itself is a dark blue, along with the four
walls. As we look to the other side of the room, we can see
some light coming through the blue curtains which hang on

the window beside the bed. The bed is covered with a red and black spread. On the top of the bed are a couple of dirty socks which look as though they have been thrown there. As we flick off the light, this sloppy situation is eliminated.

The Bedroom [white version]

The bedroom is dark blue in color. It has one window and a door. The door leads to an outside porch. In one corner there is an old brown chair. Clothes are neatly piled on the chair. Above the chair are two shelves. These shelves are lined up with books from end to end. Up against one wall is the dresser. The dresser seems to be fairly new, but the drawers are open and clothes are hanging out. On top of the dresser is a tape player with two speakers, one at each end. Along side the dresser is an old radiator which is painted light blue. The radiator does not have a cover on it. Against the other wall is the bed. The bed has a black and red spread neatly covering it. On the right side of the bed is a night-stand. Inside the nightstand are some old magazines. On the top of the stand is a lamp which is plugged into an outlet on the wall. The shade on the lamp is supposed to be white but has turned a light yellow because of its age. Directly above the bed is a round light connected to the ceiling. A shiny chrome plate surrounds the light to give it a decorative look. The light switch for this light is right next to the door through which you enter the room. There is a shiny plate covering the wires so you cannot get shocked. This room in general has a very _____ [Here I omitted a word. What word seems to belong here?] atmosphere.

While my students read and arranged the papers in the order in which they felt they had been written, I put the six possible orders of composition on the board so that we could compare and discuss our impressions. I obtained responses from three groups of writing students:

1. students in a developmental composition course, labeled here "Developmental Fall"
2. students in a regular composition course, only a few of whom had been obliged or advised to take the developmental course during the summer term, labeled here "Regular Fall"
3. students in a regular composition course, most of whom had taken the developmental course during the previous term, labeled here "Regular Winter"

Students ordered the three versions in rather different ways as shown in Table 1. The last sequence—white, blue, yellow—

represents the actual order of composition. Looking more closely at these results, we can determine the frequency with which each class placed each composition in its correct slot (Table 2).

Clearly there was enough difference of opinion, particularly in the developmental class, to warrant discussion of the relative merits of the papers and of our goals for descriptive writing. We also needed to discover what words students had used to fill in the blank in the white version. Word choices in one class included *bland, familiar, messy, bleak,* and *neat.* Those who suggested *bland* and *familiar* were the first to note that it was probably wasted effort to organize an entire composition around such un-promising ideas. While some details clearly supported the other choices, other details made them seem unlikely. The variety of answers seemed to indicate that the essay lacked coherence and focus. In fact, the writer seemed to have remembered the need for a topic sentence and, more important, a controlling idea, only as he concluded. Revelation of the original word, *gloomy,* did little to make the composition seem more coherent. If there was some-thing gloomy about a neat black and red bedspread or a chrome plate, it did not come through in the paper. Interestingly, no stu-dent in the developmental course believed that this version repre-sented the final revision, but a few in the regular classes did. Discussion revealed that the mere mention of numerous items and colors had led a few to believe that the composition was de-tailed in the way called for in the assignment. The fact that it

Table 1

Sequencing of Three Revisions of the Same Paper by Three Classes

Sequence	Developmental fall (18)		Regular fall (43)		Regular winter (34)		Total (95)	
	no.	%	no.	%	no.	%	no.	%
yellow, blue, white	0	0	2	5	0	0	2	2
blue, yellow, white	0	0	1	2	2	6	3	3
yellow, white, blue	3	17	2	5	5	15	10	11
white, yellow, blue	5	28	0	0	7	21	12	13
blue, white, yellow	8	44	26	60	1	3	35	37
white, blue, yellow	2	11	12	28	19	56	33	35

read almost like an inventory had not seemed especially negative to them. Students in all classes objected to the monotonous style of the white version, noting the succession of short, simple sentences, the allocation of one item to a sentence, and the high degree of repetition. A few observed that the writer belabored the obvious: it might be worth telling us that the lamp was not plugged in, but not that it was. By this time it was becoming clear that, in my estimation at least, this version was the least successful paper; it was the student's first effort. Among students judged to be more ready for college writing than many of their peers, however, only twenty-eight percent had found this version to be the least well developed.

Turning to the blue version, students noticed the attempt to formulate a topic sentence early in the composition. Asked whether outside of an English class they would have gone on to read a composition that began with "My bedroom is a very plain and simple room," students admitted that they would not. One student noted that the title had changed from the impersonal "The Bedroom" to "My Bedroom," and that this change was accompanied by the inclusion of more interesting and personal details. Proper nouns like Rocky and the Eagles also helped readers to visualize the room more clearly than they had been able to do in the first version. Students commented on the general improvement in sentence structure. They no longer felt as though they were being lulled to sleep or written down to, nor did they feel that the writer had struggled quite so much to get from one idea to the next. Having discussed the improved details, students now concluded that the room was not such a plain room after all. The writer had achieved a victory of sorts, but the paper still did not hold together. In fact, once again we found evidence that the writer made a final effort to announce his main idea just as he con-

Table 2

Percentage of Students Correctly Sequencing Each Version

Version	Developmental fall	Regular fall	Regular winter	Total
white	39	28	76	47
blue	11	33	56	37
yellow	56	88	59	72

cluded his essay. Had he gone back and rewritten the entire essay with this new idea in mind, the ploy might have worked. The absense of strong sensory details and the bland opening sentence seemed to explain why thirty-seven percent of the students took the blue version to be the first draft and the white version to be the second.

Now it was clear that white, blue, yellow was the order of composition. Since fewer than sixty percent of the students who were either taking developmental writing at the time or had taken it the term before believed that the yellow version was the final and best draft (as opposed to eighty-eight percent of those who had entered in the regular writing sequence), we had some differences to explore and reconcile, if possible. Students pointed out several shortcomings in the yellow version that had kept them from rating it as the final and most successful version. Some felt that the sentence patterns, while more complex than those found in the other two versions, were even more annoyingly repetitious. Others objected to the repeated comparisons of the room to a junkyard or storage room, feeling that the writer was either working too hard to fill the page or was not giving the reader enough credit for remembering what had already been read. Curiously, however, a number of students who said they found this version the most interesting of the three still did not believe that it would have been judged most favorably by the instructor because the writer did not open with a formal topic sentence. Others observed that the writer seemed to be telling a story of sorts and feared that this was incompatible with the descriptive task. Typically, these students chose the blue version, dull as they felt it was, as the best paper. What impressed students most about the yellow version was the satisfying ending; they were quick to point out how it answered the opening, explained the details in the paper, and gave the reader an insight into the character of the narrator.

Perhaps the greatest value in this exercise is the evidence it provides that revision is possible, that it is work, but certainly not a task beyond the ability and imagination of any member of the class. It also demonstrates that revision is not always a simple forward movement; in the opinion of a good number of readers, the essay got worse before it got better. The results of the in-class ranking suggest that our advice on writing is often taken more seriously (or at least more literally) than we may want it to be. The exercise itself, however, may encourage students to value their own good sense about what is and is not interesting writing.

In any case, it allows students and instructors to examine their own and one another's criteria for writing in an atmosphere that is open and exploratory, not clouded at the moment with the need to give, and to get, a grade.

Notes

1. I am grateful to my former student William Stone for permission to use his writing in the classroom and in this article.

The Delphi Technique:
Revising as Problem Solving

Robert J. Denn
Michigan State University

In *The Medusa and the Snail*, Lewis Thomas suggests that committee meetings accomplish little because human beings are too
concerned with self-image.[1] Because of this concern, he argues,
committee members spend more time thinking of impressive
things to say than they do listening, and consequently, no one
really learns anything or changes anyone else's mind. As I read
on, it occurred to me that, in this particular at least, college composition classes function like Thomas's committee meetings; students evaluate and respond to each other's writing, but often
there is little communication because the writer's attention is
engaged in controlling the nervousness that comes with being
on the spot. Having students discuss writing in small groups
alleviates the problem somewhat, if only because the instructor
is reduced to the status of *ex officio* member, but the impulse—
Thomas would say the need—to assert or defend the self-image
never entirely goes away.

Thomas does, however, describe one innovative attempt to
reduce the noise of self-assertion that drowns out the orderly
discussion of committee business. In the 1960s, the Rand Corporation developed the Delphi technique, which abolishes the committee meeting altogether and substitutes a system by which
members handle committee work in writing. Each member prepares a written response to the problem in question; these are
duplicated, and copies of all responses are then distributed to all
members. After they have had time to read and digest the ideas of
their colleagues, members sit down a second time and prepare a
revised response to the original problem, and again the responses
are duplicated and distributed. Theoretically, the process can be
repeated any number of times, but Thomas reports that after
about three rounds each member has refined his or her position as
much as is likely. These positions, however, are often more bal-

anced and more comprehensive than those presented in committee reports generated through meetings, and the reason, Thomas suggests, is that the real work went on in the quiet of an office or a study where there were fewer distractions and less interference than in a conference room during a meeting. The key to the success of the method is the reduction of noise, both the actual noise of people talking and the metaphoric noise of self-assertion.

I would like to propose a variation on the Delphi technique as one solution to the problem of unprofitable noise in the composition class. Three preliminary considerations tend to justify the attempt. First, a significant feature of the Delphi method is that it is a written mode and not an oral one, and so its use reinforces the goals of a writing course. Second, the Delphi technique as described by Thomas is relatively easy to adapt to the purposes of a composition class. And finally, Norman N. Holland and Murray Schwartz have already reported success in adapting the method for graduate seminars in literature.[2]

The Delphi technique was originally developed as a method for solving problems, and at the Rand Corporation that was how it was used; however, the approach can be adapted to a composition class if we define the problem to be solved as the construction of an effective essay. The initial student response to this problem takes the form of a rough draft; whether this draft is the result of a specific writing assignment or whether its subject and purpose originate entirely with the student are less important considerations than the student's awareness that this draft must fulfill the expectations it necessarily gives rise to in the assumed audience. Stated simply, an acceptable solution to the problem defined above is an essay that communicates something significant and specific to a particular audience, in this case the rest of the class. Once each student has a working draft, the Delphi process can begin.

In class, students exchange drafts with one another and carefully read each other's work. As they read, they note their reactions to the essay in the margins, keying their comments to broad rhetorical considerations like content, focus, organization, and development. When they finish reading an essay, they append a note in which they make specific suggestions for improvement. As soon as a student finishes reading and responding to a draft, he or she shops around for someone else who has just finished; these two then exchange drafts and continue reading. Again students make comments and suggestions, but beginning with this second round their responses are influenced by the responses of those who have read the draft previously. In the course of a fifty-minute class period, each student can read and respond to three or four first drafts.

At the end of class, drafts are returned to their authors. Each student then takes his or her paper home to consider what other students thought and to revise and rewrite it for the next class period. In most cases, especially early in the term, the single Delphi session is enough to focus the attention of students on the individual features of their writing that need the most work. Later in the term, however, follow-up Delphi sessions on revised rough drafts are valuable; in these sessions the instructor can ask student-readers to key their responses to more particular elements of writing. So, for example, students might be required to provide alternative wordings for sentences they find awkward or unclear, or they might suggest the insertion of transitions where they are needed. These essays can then be taken home, again studied and again revised. These revised essays are the ones that are ultimately typed and submitted to the instructor.

This method of peer response, then, incorporates the central feature of the original Rand Corporation technique; the level of noise is reduced, yet the members of the class continue working together toward the common goal of more effective writing. Students read the responses of their colleagues privately in their rooms or in the library where the threat of public embarrassment is reduced or eliminated, and so they concentrate more attentively on the substance of those responses. Since the comments that students write on each other's papers are more in the nature of private communications than of public pronouncements, there is greater motivation for students to be helpful rather than clever. The fact that the Delphi responses are written in class rather than at home is also important. In the past I have asked students to take each other's papers home for commentary, but the results have always been unsatisfactory, perhaps because the exercise strikes students as busywork that the instructor will never see or evaluate. (Collecting these home evaluations does little to alleviate the problem because it forces students to shift their audience from colleague to instructor and so renders the idea that the responses are communications between students something of a fiction.) By asking students to respond in class, I shift the emphasis from quantity to quality—they do not have to respond to all the essays, but they have to respond well to those for which they have time.

The results of my use of the Delphi technique in composition classes have so far been heartening. First, students have told me that they find the method helpful—some say it is the best feature of the course. They have even instituted a variation of their own, and instead of simply bringing in rough drafts, they bring in lists of questions about their drafts to direct the readers' attention to problems the writers perceive about their own work. So, for example, one student might write in the margin of her draft that she doesn't like her opening sentence, but can't think of a better one; another student doubts whether he has provided enough background information and asks his readers to tell him what, if anything, he needs to add. Second, I have observed an improvement in the quality of the essays students submit. The Delphi technique, of course, is not magic, and the familiar comma faults, bizarre spellings, and poorly developed paragraphs do not disappear overnight—in some cases there is no evidence that they will disappear at all. But because the Delphi method emphasizes that writing is communication and that readers count, I see signs that my students are trying to make their essays clear and interesting. As time goes on, I receive fewer and fewer essays characterized by unfocused or elliptical thinking, partially, I suspect, a result of asking students to respond thoughtfully to what they read in Delphi sessions. In any event, I am frequently told by students about halfway through the term that when they sit down to write, they now begin by asking themselves what will be effective, not what the instructor might want.

Notes

1. Lewis Thomas, *The Medusa and the Snail: More Notes of a Biology Watcher* (New York: Viking Press, 1979).

2. Norman N. Holland and Murray Schwartz, "The Delphi Seminar," *College English* 36 (March 1975): 789-800.

Revision and Risk

John J. Ruszkiewicz
University of Texas at Austin

Donald M. Murray opens a thought-provoking article on the revision process by observing that "writing is rewriting."[1] Many student writers would agree, appending a qualification of their own: rewriting is risky. And the more significant the revision undertaken, the greater that risk. The risk follows from the relationship between two words that circumscribe and define revision: choice and change.

If revision were entirely a matter of modifying a complete discourse or text to fit a particular situation, audience, and set of conventions, then we could define revision temporally as the act that occurs at the final stage of the composing process.[2] Indeed, traditional paradigms of composing treat revision in just this way, placing it after prewriting and writing on a linear scale. What Murray suggests, however, is that revising is an integral part of the creative process, not just the tidying up that is needed afterward:

> *Internal revision.* Under this term, I include everything writers do to discover and develop what they have to say, beginning with the reading of a completed first draft. They read to discover where their content, form, language, and voice have led them. They use language, structure, and information to find out what they have to say or hope to say. The audience is one person: the writer.[3]

Murray clings to a sequential paradigm of composing that begins with *prevision* (a step that links prewriting to preliminary choices about titles and leads), moves into *vision* (which produces a full "discovery" draft), and then into *revision*. Murray's model differs from traditional paradigms in that for him revision is no longer a terminal stage, but a point of departure. As writers revise, they discover what they really intend to say and become more conscious of the choices available to them for developing a subject.

Not all writers defer revision until after the completion of a discovery draft however. Some face their moments of significant choice earlier, at the paragraph or sentence levels, where they concentrate on those units, recasting them in various ways until they serve the writer's purpose. Writers who compose paragraph by paragraph or sentence by sentence may not produce a certifiable draft or full text for days. And despite the labored composition, the completion of this first version does not mark the completion of the essay. Yet this draft will differ significantly from one produced by the full draft method. Major revision will have occurred appreciably before the time set for its appearance by Murray's prevision-vision-revision model. While writing an initial full draft may reasonably be defended as the more inventive and productive method of composing, some writers do successfully compose paragraph by paragraph or sentence by sentence, and their acts of internal revision do occur at points prior to the presentation of a complete text. Hence their behavior must be accounted for by the admission that significant revision can occur at any stage in the composing process.

What happens as we push the revision process back into the composing act—or, perhaps more accurately, as we grow accustomed to composing paradigms that operate recursively—is that the act of revision begins to meld with the concept of invention. We discover that revisions—especially those Murray describes as internal—are no more than rhetorical choices exercised. What distinguishes an original component from a revised one is priority. The writer substitutes one choice for another. Sometimes the second choice develops from the initial one, incorporating aspects of it. In some cases, the second (or third or fourth . . .) choice is more informed than the first. It may draw from a more complete concept of what the final argument or development will be like, from more accurate information, from a heightened sense of tone and rhythm. In some cases, the revised choice will be more conventional than an initial one, the writer more carefully adjusting language to the expectations of an intended audience. But because the most rhetorically significant decisions a writer makes are likely to present the largest number of options, it is possible that second, third, or fourth choices may be no better than initial ones. They may be worse. What choice implies is what every student and teacher knows: revision does not guarantee improvement.

What revision does guarantee is change. At first glance, it might appear that change is most likely to occur when a writer is confronted by an array of potential choices. But I would suggest that just the opposite is true. While an awareness of choices in a given writing situation might ideally provoke a student to reconsider and respond, in actual practice it often does not.

The classic lament of teachers who require students to revise essays already marked and graded is that students seem to fix upon the most insignificant errors and ignore the substantial ones. Nancy Sommers has observed that many students conceive of revision as chiefly the altering and improving of vocabulary.[4] They focus on individual words, the altering of which will produce few additional changes in the discourse as a whole. The goal of their revision process seems to be to isolate areas of change within the tightest confines possible. We might attribute this entirely predictable behavior to laziness or to a lack of concern for the larger issues of development, structure, and concinnity the teacher has addressed in the marginal and final comments. Yet it is more likely and vastly more important pedagogically to consider that these students may simply be playing the odds, plotting the incentive for change against the choices available to them and going with the sure bets.

The so-called "mechanicals" present students with relatively few choices. A misspelled word, for example, guarantees a return on the time invested in correcting it. So do most reconsiderations of grammar and punctuation, which can be checked by thumbing through a handbook. Word choice, too, is largely controllable by recourse to dictionaries and thesauruses. Even some larger discourse components can be altered with surety. A student who realizes in retrospect that he or she has provided three distinct reasons for rejecting a proposal may choose to reshape the thesis in a way that anticipates this tripart development. And the student may go on to add appropriate transitions to the subsequent paragraphs: first of all, secondly, thirdly. Whenever students can clearly define and limit the choices available in a given writing situation and can discern a compelling reason for preferring one choice over others, then they are likely to alter their texts.

When the available choices are numerous and the likelihood of success less certain, an innate conservatism takes hold. Students —like most writers—regard what they have produced as an investment. Changes threaten that investment. Most writers would rather salvage a sentence already penned than write a new one, even when composing a new sentence would take less time than reshaping the old one. When advised by a teacher to reconsider the structure of an essay, to modify a thesis, to add a paragraph, to alter the predominant tone, students face situations in which recommended changes may not improve the text at all. They may lessen its effectiveness. And students do not feel sufficiently confident to make these judgments on their own. When the text in question has already been marked by the teacher, and the marginal comments include indications of mechanical failure, students will make the certain cosmetic alterations, and gamble that they will suffice. Structural, thematic, and other "major" difficulties that require revision may receive attention when students are under severe grading pressures. But if the text has been adequately, though not enthusiastically, received, students may choose to bear the ills they have rather than risk new ones.

How does a teacher counter the tendency of writers to minimize risk in the process of revising? In at least three ways: by actively teaching revision, by *not* marking mechanical errors in ways that draw undue attention to them, and by avoiding assignments that minimize risk and choice.

The first recommendation brings students closer to understanding that writing and revising are parallel and complementary processes that move writers toward language that appropriately addresses a particular situation. Certainly, students must be assured (not just told) that most writing situations generate many different yet appropriate responses. Among the classroom strategies that help are those that emphasize the process of writing, that encourage commentary and criticism before an essay is completed and graded, and that validate risk.

Since it is likely that a good deal of revision will occur after essays have been graded, students ought not to be given the impression that their work has been judged on the basis of grammar and spelling (unless, of course, that is the case). The instructor's comments should focus on the major areas in need of reconsideration, perhaps to the exclusion of all other remarks. The comments might also suggest some of the potentially effective choices open to writers, thereby encouraging revision by lessening some of the risk. Under no circumstances should an instructor attempt to justify a low grade by circling every misspelled word and comma splice, for this procedure will encourage the writer to focus on these surface matters to the exclusion of more substantive changes.

Finally, students should learn how to choose and change by doing the kinds of writing that require choice at the most difficult and risky levels. The tendency of some instructors to assign "practical" writing is—in part—an inclination to minimize the risks and choices students face in composing essays that require them to think and explore. While practical writing may produce students capable of completing job applications and preparing resumes, it may deny them the skills and confidence they need to face writing situations that require more than blanks to be filled and boxes to be checked. We should not abandon the discursive essay because Johnny is not destined to write them in the "real" world. We should leave that option and that risk to him.

Notes

1. Donald M. Murray, "Internal Revision: A Process of Discovery," in *Research in Composing: Points of Departure,* eds. Charles R. Cooper and Lee Odell (Urbana, Ill.: National Council of Teachers of English, 1978), p. 85.

2. A complete discourse or text is not necessarily a "finished" or "polished" one—though it may be. See James Kinneavy, *A Theory of Discourse* (Englewood Cliffs, N.J.: Prentice-Hall, 1971), pp. 22-23 for a discussion of the relationship of complete texts to the concept of discourse.

3. Murray, p. 91.

4. Nancy Sommers, "Revision Strategies of Experienced Writers and Student Writers" (Paper delivered at the convention of the Modern Language Association, December 28, 1978).

"But It's Just My Opinion": Understanding Conflict with Students about the Expression of Opinion

Edmund Miller
C. W. Post Center, Long Island University

One problem that often interferes with the willingness of students to take to heart the comments that writing instructors make on their papers is suspicion, sometimes a settled belief, that their instructors are merely in disagreement with them about the subjects on which they are writing. Students readily concede that they make errors in spelling and punctuation, but many seem unaware that their expression might be improved to convey more clearly and convincingly the points they want to make.

A student recently came to me after I had returned a set of papers and complained that I should not make "personal remarks" on student papers. I should not object to a student's ideas, she added, pointing to the comment that had offended her: "Though what I think you want to say seems entirely reasonable, some of the phrasing in this paper is so unidiomatic that I can't be sure." She had read a criticism of her writing as a criticism of her values. As I recall, the thesis of the paper was somewhat specious, but I had not mentioned that and had, I felt, accorded it the sacrosanct treatment she thought it merited.

Perhaps most of our students tend to see us as judge rather than guide, but students at what we might call the advanced remedial level (those who know most of the conventions of literacy but who cannot yet compose structured prose) are particularly apt to resent the judging they attribute to us. One device I have found helpful in getting such students to see that I am objecting to their failure to express ideas fully and cogently and not to their system of values is to list in parallel columns objections based on logic and those that might be made to the ideas or values in a passage from a student paper. A typical problem passage might run as follows:

> There is much more to a salesman's greeting than the words "May I help you." For example, in the store where I work

salesmen are told the greeting is an important element of
successful selling technique.

Of course, what the instructor writes in the margin varies with
circumstances—when during the semester the paper was written,
the commonness of the problem in this student's work and in the
class as a whole, even instructor fatigue affects what a student is
told. A typical teacher's response might go like this:

What is there to a greeting besides the greeting? You follow
up only by repeating that a greeting *is* important.

The problem is partly that the student has mislabeled the transition between the two sentences and thus failed to pursue the
original point. In essence, the objection is that the sequence of
ideas as presented is illogical.

Unfortunately, only a basically competent writer who has made
what is for him or her an atypical oversight could benefit from
such an abstract analysis of the problem, and the students who
object to our criticism of their ideas do not understand this objection to illogicality. When they come to our offices to argue, they
say that *we* "just do not understand the importance of a salesman's greeting." But this, they fail to see, is precisely the problem:
they have not *made us* see the importance of a salesman's greeting. If we are so rash as to tell them this, they fail to see the
irony. It is, therefore, sometimes useful to put in writing a baldly
stated opinion of the sort the student imagines us to hold:

I don't think greetings influence customers much.

When logical objections are put side by side in writing with
opinion, students begin to see the distinction, especially if the first
passionate hurt of a surprising F or D or C has passed. It is
important to put the two reactions in writing because the problem
originally arose as a result of student unfamiliarity with the
structured continuity readers expect to find in writing.

Of course, a few students remain unconvinced by this procedure, no matter how carefully carried out or how frequently repeated. Such recalcitrance, however, often goes hand in hand
with a few special subjects on which feelings tend to be heated.
I have more than once been told, for example, that "when performed by a doctor under hospital conditions abortion is not
dangerous to mother or child." To explain to the writer that
abortion is by its very nature fatal to the child is to make no headway at all—even when that objection is carefully distinguished

from remarks like "But abortion is still morally wrong." Even when such value-based objections are written in parallel columns with the logical objections and big *Xs* are run through the objections based on values, many students continue to believe that their values are under attack and leave the conference muttering unhappily, "But it's just my opinion!" They remain oblivious to the fact that the instructor has revealed no personal values whatever on the question of abortion—or capital punishment or the draft or women's liberation. The problem is that such issues are so emotionally charged for many people that they literally cannot pay attention to anything except the ethical question—even to the logical exposition of their own values.

Papers written on highly controversial topics are, therefore, of little use in helping students master the composing process, and I suggest that such subjects be banned in freshman composition. Not only should instructors not assign or list these subjects among suggested topics, but they should go further and prohibit writing on subjects that create this emotional block—even when students are eager to write on them. In an advanced course in argumentation, the issue can be confronted directly, and students taught to give the same logical coherence to presentations of their favorite positions as they require from presentations with which they take issue. But in freshman composition there are too many problems to allow us to deal adequately with this less central issue. At any rate, students in beginning writing courses are often not capable of confronting this issue in their writing.

Another way to resolve what appears to students as value conflict is to ask students for an explicit statement of the limitations they are putting on a discussion. Students may be required to incorporate (and identify) such statements within their papers, though this may be needlessly artificial, or they can be asked to turn in such statements with their completed papers, perhaps routinely as part of a checklist that includes intended audience, rhetorical mode, and the like. If students are to revise or rewrite their papers, it may be best to ask for this statement at the time of revision, for it is only then that the instructor is able to phrase the request in a way that students are likely to understand. The student who writes, for example, that "there are two kinds of Jews, Orthodox and Conservative" can be asked, "What about Reform?" The student who is an Orthodox Jew may react by saying, "Reform Jews aren't real Jews." The point the instructor needs to make, however, is that this characterization of Reform Jews as "not really Jews" has to get into the body of the paper:

the exclusion may be reasonable enough if made explicit, but since it is not obvious, it cannot be assumed. Similarly, a student may write, "Apart from the cost of accommodations, staying in a hotel is more expensive than camping out because when you stay in a hotel you have to pay for meals, laundry, and tips." The instructor may respond, "If you want to eat, you have to pay— whether you're staying in a hotel or camping out. To do your own cooking on a camping trip, you have to bring along food and cooking equipment." The student should be reassured that it is perfectly reasonable to say it is more expensive to eat in hotels than to eat on a camping trip. If the student understands the revision project, the final paper will include the idea, missing from the original paper but probably intended, that it is relatively cheaper to do a lot of things yourself and that you are unable to do them for yourself when you stay in a hotel.

Sometimes the problem is less that students have failed to express ideas completely than that they have failed to pursue what they wanted to say long enough to see the point themselves. The following is a case of this sort: "Christmas is being commercialized nowadays. The true meaning of Christmas depends on how much feeling you put into the gifts you give, not on how much they cost." For the instructor merely to note, "Oh, I don't think giving has gotten so very out of hand" will have little effect. A longer reaction is likely to run along the following lines: "Hasn't Christmas been commercial for a long, long time? And while gift giving doesn't have to be commercial, it is necessarily a *secular* idea and one that is therefore only tenuously related to the 'true meaning of Christmas.'" Yet such a reaction, if the instructor takes the time to write it out in full, is usually not understood by the student for what it is—a serious attempt to understand what was intended. The response that works best in such cases is to ask the student to state the assumptions implicit in the original passage: "When did commercialization begin? What is the true meaning of Christmas?" Even so, if we do not want the student to think us perverse or nitpicking, such questions can usually be asked only in conferences, and thus the process will be a time-consuming one. With noncontroversial material of this sort, however, it is often possible to enable students to see how much needs to be clarified in their own thinking before their ideas can take shape as lucid prose.

A similar difficulty is presented in this passage: "The Salem witch trials were the most inhumane episode in the history of civilization." When better students produce material that is so absurdly hyperbolic, a baldly ironic comment in the margin may suffice. With most hyperbolists, however, a conference is called for. The huge numbers who died in the Nazi concentration camps, in the Reign of Terror, in Tamerlane's conquest of India would have to be contrasted with the numbers who died in Colonial New England. And the fact that most of those accused at Salem were not convicted and most of those convicted were not executed would have to be mentioned. Unless the instructor has a reference book handy, he or she may not be believed, so a better solution is to make a research project out of the problem:

> Find, giving complete bibliographical citations for your sources:
> 1. the number of people who stood trial at Salem
> 2. the number convicted at Salem
> 3. the number executed as witches in Colonial New England
> 4. the number who died in Nazi concentration camps
> 5. the number who died in Tamerlane's conquests

Some students may resent such assignments, but they also learn a lot from them about how to find and use evidence and even about how to temper their expression. But this last valuable effect may come about only if the instructor arranges a follow-up conference. We have with this passage come close to one of those rare occasions when an instructor does rightly object to what a student is saying. Even so, we have not actually done so, and if a student having put the full facts before us did wish to argue that the execution of twenty people in a moment of cultural hysteria in Colonial New England was more inhumane than the systematic executions of tens of thousands in the ovens of Auschwitz, we would maintain privately the strongest reservations about that student's maturity and common sense—but we would probably say nothing.

Another passage from the witch trial paper provides a contrast because we do object when the writer says, "After hearing testimony consisting of nothing more than wild accusations, the Salem judges condemned thousands to be burned at the stake." This is simply an error of fact, and we write, "In all, twenty were hanged at Salem. No one was burned, and many of the accused were, in fact, acquitted." Again a research assignment—with documentation—is the best solution for the problem.

Problems such as these, I might add, are entirely gratuitous in my composition classes since I do not assign topics that fall outside student experience. Nevertheless, some students rewrite the assignments in order to introduce such topics, sometimes because they are lazy and have the material prepared for another course—or think they do. But the difficulty may, in fact, be more serious. Students often seem to think that anything they know they know firsthand, when in fact most knowledge comes to them from books and lectures and other organized reference sources. And of course the difficulty is compounded when, as in the witch trials instance, the material has come to them in garbled form.

Consider, for a moment, an example from another student paper: "The people of Columbus's time thought the world was flat." The instructor's reaction goes something like this: "This is one of the myths of our time. Europeans of Columbus's day knew the world to be round. In fact, the Ptolemaic system of astronomy that Copernicus and Galileo had so much trouble in overthrowing is founded on the principle of a round earth." Yet, such myths are hard to dispel—even professional writers sometimes confuse the dark side of the moon, the face we never see, with the half of the moon that happens to be in darkness. But such material is seldom the sort that involves students emotionally, and a frank discussion in class may not only clear the air but also make clear that it is no help in such cases for students to introduce erroneous ideas with a ritual disclaimer like "I feel that..." Such disclaimers have no power to change the facts. Students who "feel" that the people of Columbus's day believed the world to be flat are merely misinformed. Telling us that they believe erroneous information may give us an interesting insight into their psychology, but the response of any informed person has to be, "But you are mistaken." In cases of factual error, the instructor rightly objects that a student's feelings and opinions are quite beside the point.

When an instructor feels it is important for students to practice argumentation in freshman composition, he or she must bring to their attention the need to treat all sides of an issue. This point should be discussed in class before the argumentative assignment, for students often think it is enough to argue for or against an issue and fail to distinguish the evenhanded treatment of the several sides of an argument (which is not required) from dealing with and explaining away the arguments most likely to be raised by proponents of a position they choose not to support. Few students at this stage have skill in rebuttal. Many will not immediately appreciate the need to answer opponents, even after preliminary lectures, so a class session spent generating the arguments that might be presented by each side on an issue (certainly a nonemotional one for best results) is useful in illustrating how the arguments of each side might be dealt with by proponents of another. And such treatment should be explicitly distinguished from giving equal credence to conflicting points of view.

I prefer, however, to omit argument entirely in freshman composition. While it is true that much college writing has an argumentative cast to it, almost all college writing—and almost all general postgraduate writing—is basically expository. Freshman composition students have many real difficulties with the rhetoric of exposition that need to be dealt with first, while many of the special problems they have with argumentation result from a lack of knowledge or inexperience with the subject matter at hand that can only be resolved by far more elaborate research projects of the sort I have already suggested. Teaching freshman composition is enough work without manufacturing difficulties. Instead, I try to keep before me the healthy suspicion that many of my students still sometimes think I merely disagree with them when in fact what I continue to want is for them to write more clearly. Unless I keep their misapprehension before me and continue to use special strategies to deal with it, I will not be able to help them express themselves more clearly, and any revising I require will be an exercise in futility.

Empathy and Re-vision

Karen I. Spear
University of Utah

Professional writers agree that revision is the most important part of writing. John Updike speaks for many when he says, "Writing and rewriting are a constant search for what one is saying."[1] Teachers of writing usually recognize the wisdom of this statement and attempt to encourage revision. But regardless of what they say about the virtues of revising, they typically attach little real significance to revisions, treating them as something students should do for their own good but for little credit, or as punishment for or reprieve from a bad grade. Students, responding to what their teachers do rather than what they say about revising, rarely make more than cosmetic changes in otherwise finished products.

Clearly, what Updike means by revising and what students do about it are very different. Thus, teachers need to bring students closer to the ideal that Updike suggests—a re-vision not of the presentation of ideas in words, sentences, and paragraphs but of the ideas themselves. Students need to learn how to sustain their "vision" and how to continue to explore it throughout the writing process.

One way for teachers to encourage this sustained vision is to practice a fundamental principle of communication: people understand what they mean largely through the understanding they receive from others; or, as another writer puts it, "To understand himself man needs to be understood by another."[2] Effective communication derives from the interaction between persons generating ideas and the audiences responding to them—the continual questioning, clarifying, exploring, agreeing, and disagreeing that must transpire for people to understand each other and themselves. James Moffett calls this process "feedback and response," the kind of interaction between novice and coach that promotes the learning of any skill. As Moffett points out, "In learning to use language the only kind of feedback available to us is human response."[3] Interaction through feedback and response, then, tends to foster re-vision in the literal sense of the word.

When teachers provide feedback, they are rehearsing ideas with students, trying to see them as students do, giving students their reflection of what the ideas mean and how they work. In this respect, the teacher, as surrogate audience, acts much like the therapist who serves as a surrogate society, mirroring the meaning and effects of a client's behavior. In both cases, important re-visions occur.

The Value of Empathy

A therapist's ability to think with another person, to assume that person's perspective on a topic, is called empathy. Recognized as the *sine qua non* of successful therapy, regardless of the kind of therapy, empathy is the foremost characteristic of a relationship in which clients feel free to think about and articulate problems, ambiguities, or paradoxes not easily expressed. Empathic responses convey the message, "I understand you; I see the issue as you see it, in all its complexity." At the highest level, empathic communication reflects the therapist's awareness of more than the surface meaning of the client's statements. Such deeply empathic responses, according to Charles Truax and Robert Carkhuff, two of the foremost researchers on effective therapy, elaborate the client's verbal, gestural, and contextual implications into "full-blown, sensitive, but still tentative verbalizations of feelings or experiences."[4] The more accurately the therapist reflects what the client has said, the more likely the client is to explore the topic in greater depth, refining and revising the material.

Accurate empathy depends upon two variables in the therapist's responses: frequency and specificity. Truax and Carkhuff note that the more frequently a therapist makes responses, even if only to say "I see" or to nod, the more accurately the therapist comprehends what is being said and the more likely the client is to perceive the therapist's empathy. As a result of this perception, the client pursues ideas more freely and rigorously. The more concrete and specific the therapist's responses, the more concrete and specific the client's comments. By attending to the needs for frequency and specificity, therapists force themselves to listen closely, improving their comprehension and enabling clients to correct them immediately if their perceptions are inaccurate. In

addition, clients are less likely to become too general or abstract;
when they do, the therapist's insistence on detail prompts them
to support their generalizations adequately.[5]

The communication of empathy modifies the therapist's role,
changing it from analyst to ally, from evaluator to helper. Carl
Rogers describes this more empathic role and its consequences:
"The therapist must lay aside his preoccupation with diagnosis
and his diagnostic shrewdness, must discard his tendency to
make professional evaluations, must cease his endeavors to formulate an accurate prognosis, must give up the temptation to
subtly guide the individual, and must concentrate on one purpose
only; that of providing deep understanding and acceptance of the
attitudes consciously held at a particular moment by the client as
he explores step by step into the dangerous areas which he has
been denying to consciousness."[6] In short, by assuming the role
of fellow explorer instead of omniscient authority, the empathic
therapist encourages the client's sustained re-vision in both con-
ceptualizing and expressing ideas.

The results of accurate empathy in therapy are closely related
to what we seek to bring about through the teaching of writing:
proficiency in verbalizing complex issues, in refining subtleties
in meaning, in attending to rich supporting detail, in discovering
an authentic voice, and in exploring ideas that are real and
meaningful. As Updike's comment suggests, these traits do not
come from first attempts; rather, they evolve through successive
re-visions. To the extent that teachers can express empathy, they
enable themselves to prompt such re-visions by eliciting and
sharing the student's ongoing explorations of an idea. The sus-
pension of judgments, criticisms, and evaluations inherent in
empathic communication embodies the teacher's recognition that
such responses, made prematurely, hinder comprehension and
inhibit the student's generation and refinement of thought. By
understanding how empathy contributes to communication, and
by learning how to express it, teachers can foster and expedite
genuine re-vision.

Empathic Communication

Truax and Carkhuff make an important distinction between the
experience of empathy and its expression. No matter how sensitive a therapist may be to a client, the therapist must possess
"the verbal facility to communicate this understanding in a lan-

guage attuned to the client's current feelings."[7] The same distinction between experiencing empathy and expressing it holds for teachers. Studies conducted in a variety of settings show that the ability to communicate empathically is relatively low among members of the helping professions (including teachers). Arthur Combs, for example, a researcher who has extensively investigated the relationships between counseling and teaching, reports a series of studies conducted in ten states by the National Consortium for Humanistic Education that measured the levels of empathy among elementary and secondary teachers. The data uniformly indicate that teachers generally provide levels of empathy that "tend to retard rather than facilitate learning."[8] On the other hand, as teachers learn to communicate their empathy, students significantly improve their academic progress, attendance, and even IQ scores. Rather than indicting teachers for incompetence or insensitivity, this evidence may reinforce the distinction between experiencing and expressing empathy. What teachers lack, it seems, are not empathic attitudes toward students but the ability to communicate those attitudes in ways that bring about open, sensitive, and detailed discussion.

If teachers are not as empathic as they think they are, what should they be doing that they are not? More specifically, how is empathy communicated?

The simplest form of empathic response is a paraphrase of the speaker's statement insofar as the listener understands it. Paraphrases signal that the listener has attended to the statement, is actively trying to understand it, and seeks further clarification or elaboration. Moreover, paraphrases encourage people to talk, pursuing topics in their own way but in enough detail to explain them to someone else. A student, for example, might come for a conference with only a few notes scribbled on a dog-eared page and sigh, "This is as far as I could get." In an effort to offer hearty encouragement, the teacher might respond, "Oh! You can do better than that. Your last paper was full of good ideas." Although well-intentioned, this response shifts attention from the current problem with the immediate assignment. It also puts the student on the defensive. More empathic responses would paraphrase the problem: "You feel like you're up against a brick wall"; "So far this topic doesn't seem to go anywhere"; or "You ran out of ideas." Each of these statements, conveyed in tones of understanding rather than accusation, reflects the teacher's acceptance of the student's problem. More important, each statement insists that the problem is still the student's, not the teacher's, that the issues (and the student) are worthwhile, and that the teacher is willing to act as a sounding board for further exploration of the topic's potential.

As talk progresses to the ideas themselves, the teacher who has become truly engaged in the student's thinking will be able to move to higher levels of empathy, paraphrasing surface content but also reflecting subtleties, nuances, and implications that have not fully come into the student's awareness. Responses with such intense empathy will likely be met with surprised insight and an increased sensitivity to the topic's latent potential. In his essay, "The Conditions of Creativity," Jerome Bruner calls this type of response "effective surprise," the experience of shocked recognition, "following which there is no longer astonishment."[9] At this level of communication, teachers can begin to combine questions, comments, and advice with their reflections, adding their perspective on the written product to the student's perspective on its content. Constructive criticism is more likely to be accepted in the spirit in which it is given, not, as so often happens, as either the final blow to the student's self-esteem or as a signal to the student to stop thinking because the all-knowing teacher is about to announce how to do it right. At this level, too, the teacher's nonthreatening and relatively nondirective role in the relationship will be apparent, and the student should feel free to generate and refine ideas, having accepted primary responsibility for guiding the discussion. Periodically, the teacher might also summarize what seem to be major themes in the discussion, providing a verbal and conceptual model for the principles of unity and coherence being taught in writing.

Using these techniques, teachers communicate empathy, thus modeling and eliciting the kind of sustained, critical thinking that is the foremost prerequisite for revising. In *The Relevance of Education,* Jerome Bruner clarifies the relationships among modeling, empathy, and re-vision: "The earliest form of learning essential to the person becoming human is not so much discovery as it is having a model. The constant provision of a model, the constant response to the individual's response after response, back and forth between two people, constitutes 'invention' learning guided by an accessible model."[10] Bruner's comments imply that invention plays a larger role in composition than is currently believed. When teachers are fully involved in the student's re-vision of material, invention becomes part of a spiral, not a stage in a linear sequence. Thus, invention and re-vision become virtually synonymous, different phases of the same activity, not different activities. Moreover, the presence of an empathic model keeps thought spiraling and re-vision going.

Empathy, in addition to serving the one-to-one relationship between student and teacher, is important in the classroom. A teacher who communicates empathy to the class provides a model for attending to others, conveying to the class that each speaker has something worthwhile to say. In this respect, sustained listening promotes sustained re-vision. Although much less is known about communication in groups than about communication between two people, Carl Rogers hypothesizes that "group members may gradually begin to behave toward others in the group in much the same way as the leader behaves toward them."[11] By demonstrating empathic communication to students, and by holding students to the same standards of communication that teachers demand of themselves, teachers can legitimately expect students to become better able to help their peers revise their writing. Most important, however, is that as teachers become more empathically engaged with the writing processes of their students, both individually and as a group, they demonstrate that revision is actually a series of re-visions, conceived largely through interaction with others.

As an issue in the pedagogy of writing, the need for empathy has a bearing not only on the teacher's interpersonal behavior with students, but also on the organization of the class. Primarily, the system for handling conferences and evaluating papers must reflect the teacher's commitment to sustained investigation of topics. Drafts must be recognized as drafts by students and teachers alike, and teachers must be willing to engage in empathic dialogue with students to model the process of re-vision. In addition, a revised paper must be genuinely rewarded, not regarded as a kind of booby prize for the student who couldn't get it right the first time.

I would not suggest that once we learn to convey empathy the task of teaching students to revise is finished. Nor would I try to present a model of behavior that all teachers should emulate. Just as teachers of writing assert that prose should be clear yet distinctive, so must teachers be empathic yet uniquely themselves. I would, however, assert that the problems students have with revising are cognitive on the one hand and motivational on the other: they don't know what revising is, they don't know how to do it, and they don't receive incentives to make it worthwhile. Teachers who can convey empathy have the necessary prerequisites for solving all three problems: empathic communication inspires persistent re-vision, provides a model for its accomplishment, and yields the intrinsic reward of understanding oneself and being understood.

Notes

1. Cited in Donald M. Murray, "Internal Revision: A Process of Discovery," in *Research on Composing: Points of Departure,* eds. Charles R. Cooper and Lee Odell (Urbana, Ill.: National Council of Teachers of English, 1978), p. 103.

2. Thomas Hora, "Tao, Zen and Existential Psychotherapy," *Psychologia* 2 (1959), p. 237.

3. James Moffett, *Teaching the Universe of Discourse* (Boston: Houghton Mifflin, 1968), pp. 188–89.

4. Charles B. Truax and Robert R. Carkhuff, *Toward Effective Counseling and Psychotherapy: Training and Practice* (Chicago: Aldine Publishing Co., 1967), p. 285.

5. Truax and Carkhuff, pp. 287–88.

6. Carl Rogers, *Client-Centered Therapy: Its Current Practice, Implications, and Theory* (Boston: Houghton Mifflin, 1965), p. 30.

7. Truax and Carkhuff, p. 46.

8. Arthur Combs, ed., *Humanistic Education: Objectives and Assessment* (Washington, D.C.: American Association for Supervision and Curriculum Development, 1978), p. 41.

9. Jerome Bruner, *On Knowing: Essays for the Left Hand* (New York: Atheneum, 1971), p. 18.

10. Jerome Bruner, *The Relevance of Education* (New York: W. W. Norton, 1973), p. 70.

11. Rogers, p. 348.

Bibliography

An Annotated Bibliography on Revision

Charles R. Duke
Murray State University

The articles and texts listed here were chosen for their direct concern with helping students and teachers understand what revision is and how it fits into the overall process of writing.

Arbur, Rosemarie. "The Student-Teacher Conference." *College Composition and Communication* 28 (December 1977): 338-42.

Offers suggestions for conducting effective conferences with students, based on an analogy between the conference and the "interview" as analyzed by sociologists.

Bain, Robert. "Reading Student Papers." *College Composition and Communication* 25 (October 1974): 307-9.

Lists eight key questions to ask when reading student papers; questions can be adapted easily for student use in small groups.

Beach, Richard. "The Effects of Between-Draft Teacher Evaluation versus Self-Evaluation on High School Students' Revising of Rough Drafts." *Research in Teaching English* 13 (May 1979): 111-19.

Reports that students who were provided between-draft teacher evaluations showed a greater degree of change, higher fluency, and greater differences in support of ideas on final drafts than students employing self-evaluation and students receiving no evaluation.

Beach, Richard. "Self-Evaluation Strategies of Extensive Revisers and Nonrevisers." *College Composition and Communication* 27 (May 1976): 160-64.

Notes the attitudes expressed toward revision by two groups of students, one of extensive revisers, the other of nonrevisers.

Beaven, Mary H. "Individualized Goal Setting, Self-Evaluation, and Peer Evaluation." In *Evaluating Writing: Describing, Measuring, Judging,* edited by Charles R. Cooper and Lee Odell, pp. 135–56. Urbana, Ill.: National Council of Teachers of English, 1977.

Describes procedures for teachers to use in commenting upon writing and in helping students set and achieve goals for improvement, and for students to use in peer evaluations of writing.

Benson, Nancy L. "The Effects of Peer Feedback during the Writing Process on Writing Performance, Revision Behavior, and Attitude toward Writing." Ph. D. dissertation, University of Colorado at Boulder, 1979.

Reports that the effect of peer feedback during the writing process was beneficial to junior high school students in the areas of paragraph, sentence, word, and total revision.

Beyer, Barry K. "Prewriting and Rewriting to Learn." *Social Education,* March 1979, pp. 187–89.

Describes pre- and postwriting activities designed to aid students in submitting polished papers; rewriting aspect involves evaluation, revision, and editing.

Birdsall, Eric R. "Avoiding Whadjaget with No-Grade, Graded Papers." *College Composition and Communication* 30 (May 1979): 220–22.

Offers a technique for increasing student concern for the merits of their papers and for their teacher's suggestions based on withholding the grade and offering an opportunity to rewrite.

Boiarsky, Carolyn. "Cut-and-Paste and Other Revision Activities." *English Journal* 69 (November 1980): 44–48.

Identifies and briefly describes eleven basic activities that occur during the revision process.

Bolker, Joan L. "Reflections on Reading Student Writing." *College English* 40 (October 1978): 181–85.

Suggests that teachers comment on papers in such a way as to convey that they are hearing students, not merely criticizing and judging, and thus encourage students to "feel that their writing belongs to them."

Bracher, Peter. "Rewriting and the Teaching of Composition." *Arizona English Bulletin* 21 (April 1979): 95–98.

Discusses barriers that may hinder students from engaging in useful writing activity; these barriers include grading, time for rewriting, and types of teacher comments.

Brand, Alice Glarden. "Reversing the Revision 'Blues.'" In *Activating the Passive Student*. Classroom Practices in Teaching English 1978–1979, edited by Gene Stanford, pp. 77–83. Urbana, Ill.: National Council of Teachers of English, 1978.

Offers a three-phase approach to introducing revising skills, beginning with obvious errors easily corrected by the entire class and moving toward more complex areas; students work directly with their own writing, but collaborative revising is encouraged.

Bridwell, Lillian S. "Revising Processes in Twelfth-Grade Students' Transactional Writing." Ed. D. dissertation, University of Georgia, 1979.

Describes a study of twelfth-grade student drafts of an informative/argumentative essay; surface and word levels are shown to be the most frequent units of revision, and the majority of these changes occurred during in-process stages; significant relationships between revision levels and qualitative ratings of essays are also noted.

Bridwell, Lillian S. "Revising Strategies in Twelfth-Grade Students' Transactional Writing." *Research in the Teaching of English* 14 (October 1980): 197–222.

Suggests that patterns in revision strategies exist and that these patterns are associated with writing quality.

Bruffee, Kenneth A. *A Short Course in Writing: Practical Rhetoric for Composition Courses, Writing Workshops and Tutor Training Programs.* 2d ed. Cambridge, Mass.: Winthrop Publishing Co., 1980.

Combines writing activities/assignments with explanations about collaborative writing, peer criticism and tutoring; useful suggestions about setting up a writing course in which revision is a natural activity.

Calkins, Lucy McCormick. "Notes and Comments: Children's Rewriting Strategies." *Research in the Teaching of English* 14 (December 1980): 331–41.

Describes characteristics that identify types of rewriting in the work of third-graders.

Canuteson, John. "Conferences as Evaluative Devices in Freshman Composition." Paper presented at the annual meeting of the Conference on College Composition and Communication, Kansas City, Missouri, March 1977. (ERIC Document Reproduction Service No. ED 143 027).

Recommends a procedure whereby students write during each class period and discuss their papers in weekly individual conferences with the instructor; this method allows for prompt and individualized attention, saves time in correcting papers, and seems to play a role in reducing attrition.

Champagne, Mireille and others. "Children's Problems with Focus and Cohesion in Revising." Paper presented at the annual meeting of the American Educational Research Association, Boston, Massachusetts, April 1980. (ERIC Document Reproduction Service No. ED 186 901).

Reports that the apparent lack of interest among third-, sixth-, and ninth-graders in undertaking substantial revisions may be due in part to their inability to handle aspects of focus and cohesion consistently.

Clifford, John. "Teaching Composing Collaboratively." *Arizona English Bulletin* 22 (February 1980): 95–98.

Outlines ways of gradually moving students from their perception of the teacher as single audience/respondent to seeing small writing groups as places where help can be gained for rewriting, revising, and editing.

Cooper, Charles. "Responding to Writing." In *The Writing Processes of Students: Report of the First Annual Conference on Language Arts,* edited by Walter T. Petty and Patrick J. Finn, pp. 31–39. Buffalo: State University of New York, 1975.

Offers practical suggestions for ways of responding to writing so that students will perceive possibilities for improvement in their drafts.

Cronin, Frank C. "Creative, Rhetorical, and Editorial Revisions: An Autobiographical Account." *Ohio English Language Arts Bulletin,* Winter/Spring 1980, pp. 15–18.

Provides a personal view of how revision affects the way the author writes.

Cunningham, Donald, and G. Ronald Dobler. "Teaching by the Numbers: An Exercise in Organization and Revision." *Exercise Exchange,* Fall 1977, pp. 36–40.

Suggests using previously written and revised essays to teach students about the value of revision.

Della-Piana, Gabriel M. "Research Strategies for the Study of Revision Processes in Writing Poetry." In *Research on Composing: Points of Departure,* edited by Charles R. Cooper and Lee Odell, pp. 105–34. Urbana, Ill.: National Council of Teachers of English, 1978.

Reviews previously published reports and studies and suggests research that might be attempted on how poets revise; offers a model of the revision process and suggests approaches to the study of revision that might be applied to any form of writing.

Della-Piana, Gabriel M., and George T. Endo. "Writing as Revision." Paper presented at the annual meeting of the American Educational Research Association, New York, April 1977. (ERIC Document Reproduction Service No. ED 137 791).

Views revision as a process that occurs prior to and throughout
the writing of a work until it is finished or abandoned. Outlines
a longitudinal experimental study of the process of writing as
revision.

Denman, Mary Edel. "I Got This Here Hang-up: Noncognitive
Processes for Facilitating Writing." *College Composition and
Communication* 26 (October 1975): 305–9.

Identifies procedures for helping students discover in class the
strong points in each other's writing and relates these techniques to the comments offered by the teacher in annotating
each paper.

Dudenhefer, John P., Jr. "An Experimental Study of Two Techniques of Composition Revision in a Developmental English
Course for Technical Students." Ph. D. dissertation, University
of Mississippi, 1975.

Reports a reduction in errors of grammar, usage, punctuation,
and spelling in papers of students who revised after papers
were marked but before they were graded.

Duke, Charles R. "The Student-Centered Conference and the Writing Process." *English Journal* 64 (December 1975): 44–47.

Recommends Rogerian techniques to change teacher-centered
writing conferences to student-centered ones and to place responsibility for revision with the student.

Duke, Charles R. "Responding to Student Writing." *Connecticut
English Journal* 9 (Fall 1977): 148–59.

Suggests ways for focusing student attention on the need for
revision: overhead projector, opaque projector, oral reading,
small group response, cassette response, and written comments.

Duke, Charles R. "An Approach to Revision and Evaluation of
Student Writing." *Ohio Language Arts Bulletin,* Winter 1980,
pp. 19–24.

Offers a structured approach to make revision a central part
of a writing course and, as a result, a method for diminishing
student fear of grading.

Dworsky, Nancy. "The Disaster Workshop." *College English* 35 (November 1973): 194-95.

Recommends that teachers spend their time not on writing that students consider finished but on writing that students are dissatisfied with.

Effros, Charlotte. "An Experimental Study of the Effects of Guided Revision and Delayed Grades on Writing Proficiency of College Freshmen." Final Report, National Institute of Education, U.S. Department of Health, Education, and Welfare, Grant No. OEG-72-0017(509). West Haven, Conn.: New Haven University, 1973. (ERIC Document Reproduction Service No. ED 079 764).

Reports that the control group, which used incidental revision with immediate grades, performed significantly better than did the experimental group, which had grades delayed until revisions were completed, on English Expression Tests; interaction between teacher/class and method was highly significant. There were no significant differences between groups on the essay test.

Elbow, Peter. "The Teacherless Writing Class." In *Writing without Teachers,* pp. 76-146. New York: Oxford University Press, 1973.

Outlines responsibilities that can be accepted by students in performing as respondents, editors, and critics of their own writing and that of others.

Fassler, Barbara. "The Red Pen Revisited: Teaching Composition through Student Conferences." *College English* 40 (October 1978): 186-90.

Describes a teaching method based on twenty-minute conferences with students where papers are read and evaluated and priorities for next drafts are established; papers are not read prior to conferences.

Fitzgibbon, Joseph. "Reducing the Drudgery of Correcting Compositions." *Media and Methods,* March 1980, pp. 27-29.

Suggests how to place proofreading/editing responsibilities in the hands of students.

Flanigan, Michael C., and Diane S. Menendez. "Perception and Change: Teaching Revision." *College English* 42 (November 1980): 256–66.

Describes structured revision activities that direct the approach students use in reading and reporting about their own writing and that of others at various stages.

Gentry, Larry A. "Textual Revision: A Review of the Research." Report No. SWRL-TN-2-80/11. Los Alamitos, Calif.: Southwest Regional Laboratory for Educational Research and Development, 1980. (ERIC Document Reproduction Service No. ED 192 355).

Examines the relative effectiveness of various revision strategies used by skilled and unskilled writers.

Gibson, Walker. "The Writing Teacher as a Dumb Reader." *College Composition and Communication* 30 (May 1979): 192–95.

Suggests that teachers can aid students in overcoming lack of clarity in their writing by showing them how to become more sensitive to the reader's ignorance of the writer's intentions; sample problems included.

Glavich, Sister Mary Kirene. "Writing in Circles: A Way around the Paper Problem." *Ohio Language Arts Bulletin,* Winter/Spring 1980, pp. 57–60.

Advocates the use of student-to-student evaluations within writer's circles and suggests how to prepare students to respond constructively to each other's writing.

Graves, Donald H. "Research Update: What Children Show Us about Revision." *Language Arts* 56 (March 1979): 312–19.

Presents early data on revision from a two-year study of the writing processes of sixteen primary children.

Graves, Donald H., and Lucy McCormick Calkins. "Research Update: Andrea Learns to Make Writing Hard." *Language Arts* 56 (May 1979): 569–76.

Describes a third-grader's approach to revision.

Graves, Donald H., and Donald M. Murray. "Revision in the Writer's Workshop and in the Classroom." *Journal of Education,* Spring 1980, pp. 38–56.

Provides the journal notes of a writer engaged in revision and the commentary of a researcher on the writing process.

Groff, Patrick. "Does Negative Criticism Discourage Children's Compositions?" *Language Arts* 52 (October 1975): 1032–34.

Reviews studies on the effect of negative criticism on children's compositions.

Gwyn, Cindy, and Deborah Swanson-Owens. "Essay Editing: Helping Students Teach Themselves." San Francisco, Calif.: San Francisco State University, 1980. (ERIC Document Reproduction Service No. ED 192 327).

Outlines procedures for establishing student editing groups and suggests areas for emphasis.

Hansen, Barbara. "Rewriting Is a Waste of Time." *College English* 39 (April 1978): 956–60.

Suggests that students profit more by discussing their errors in class than by rewriting and correcting their papers.

Hansen, Barbara. "Teaching Revision." *Exercise Exchange,* Fall 1978, pp. 10–15.

Offers specific guidelines for developing revision lessons; sample included.

Hardaway, Francine. "What Students Can Do to Take the Burden off You." *College English* 36 (January 1975): 577–80.

Outlines a system of peer evaluation that, when combined with teacher conferences, increases student motivation and reduces common mechanical errors.

Harris, Muriel. "Evaluation: The Process for Revision." *Journal of Basic Writing,* Spring-Summer 1978, pp. 82–90.

Suggests that extensive practice in evaluation during each writing stage from prewriting to final draft helps students sharpen their skills as critics of each other's writing, guides them as they review their own writing, and demonstrates to them that evaluating their writing is essentially their job, not the teacher's.

Hicks, Joyce. "Structured Revision Tasks." *Exercise Exchange,* Fall 1978, pp. 15-17.

Indicates how to focus student attention on revision problems of focus, tone, and style.

Hildick, Wallace. *Word for Word: The Rewriting of Fiction.* New York: W. W. Norton and Co., 1965.

Contains examples from manuscripts of Henry James, Thomas Hardy, Virginia Woolf, and others that indicate the types of revision practiced by these authors.

Ilacqua, Alma A. "'I Like It!' Doesn't Make It Good: Writing Is (A) Discipline." *Arizona English Bulletin* 22 (February 1980): 89-94.

Describes a lesson in which students learn how to make constructive critical responses to writing.

Jacko, Carol M. "Small-Group Triad: An Instructional Mode for the Teaching of Writing." *College Composition and Communication* 29 (October 1978): 290-92.

Describes a structured form of small-group discussion, called the triad, which allots specific roles that enable group members to focus on each other's drafts.

Jacobs, Suzanne E., and Adela B. Karliner. "Helping Writers to Think: The Effect of Speech Roles in Individual Conferences on the Quality of Thought in Student Writing." *College English* 38 (January 1977): 489-505.

Comments on transcripts of two interviews between teacher and student concerning the drafts of essays, focusing on the roles played by teacher and by student and the need for the teacher to perceive when roles should change.

Jones, Thelma Ludwig. "An Exploratory Study of the Impact on Student Writing of Peer Evaluation." Ph. D. dissertation, Michigan State University, 1977.

Explores the effect of peer evaluation on narrative, descriptive, and analytic writing and the development of self-initiated student changes in drafts.

Judy, Stephen M., and Susan J. Judy. "The Red Pencil Blues." In *The English Teacher's Handbook: Ideas and Resources for Teaching English,* pp. 237-47. Cambridge, Mass.: Winthrop Publishing Co., 1979.

Offers suggestions about the roles teachers can assume when responding to student writing; including those of personal respondent, manuscript manager, technical advisor, and stage director or manager; assuming such roles helps students understand how their writing should be viewed at particular stages.

Kehl, D. G. "The Art of Writing Evaluative Comments on Student Themes." *English Journal* 59 (October 1970): 972-80.

Suggests how to write marginal and summary comments that will help students improve their writing.

Keith, Philip M. "TCDIDC, A Revising Heuristic; or On beyond the Toadstool." Paper presented at the annual meeting of the Conference on College Composition and Communication, Kansas City, Missouri, March 1977. (ERIC Document Reproduction Service No. ED 147 818).

Presents a model for students to use when revising compositions; focuses on patterns of tenses and other time markers, patterns of predicate modes, directness of voice, and patterns of noun types, descriptors, and connectors. Samples of writing suggest that the use of this model leads to improvement in sentence and paragraph construction.

Kirby, Dan R., and Tom Liner. "Revision: Yes, They Do It; Yes, You Can Teach It." *English Journal* 69 (March 1980): 41-45.

Offers eight principles about revising that teachers should understand before introducing revision to students.

Knapp, John V. "Contract/Conference Evaluations of Freshman Composition." *College English* 37 (March 1976): 647-53.

Suggests a way of organizing a class so emphasis is placed on developing acceptable drafts rather than merely writing for a grade.

Koch, Carl, and James M. Brazil. *Strategies for Teaching the Composition Process.* Urbana, Ill.: National Council of Teachers of English, 1978.

Offers examples of lessons that focus student attention on various aspects of the composing process, including revision.

Krupa, Gene H. "Primary Trait Scoring in the Classroom." *College Composition and Communication* 30 (May 1979): 214-15.

Recounts a classroom experiment in which primary trait scoring was used as a basis for determining the areas to be addressed by students in revising their papers.

Lagana, Jean R. "The Development, Implementation, and Evaluation of a Model for Teaching Composition Which Utilizes Individualized Learning and Peer Grouping." Ph. D. dissertation, University of Pittsburgh, 1972.

Reports that peer evaluation tended to be as effective as teacher corrections and allowed students to complete more compositions and to receive more feedback on each.

Lamberg, Walter J. "Feedback on Writing: Much More Than Teacher Corrections." *Statement: The Journal of the Colorado Language Arts Society,* May 1977, pp. 33-38.

Defines *feedback* as "information about performance," reviews various theories about responding to student writing, cites the results of related research, and asks whether feedback should be different for different purposes and conditions.

Lamberg, Walter J. "Self-provided and Peer-provided Feedback." *College Composition and Communication* 31 (February 1980): 63-69.

Argues that responses from peers and teachers can be supplemented by writers providing their own feedback about what they have written.

Lanham, Richard A. *Revising Business Prose.* New York: Charles Scribner's Sons, 1981.

Offers a "paramedic method" as a self-teaching revision technique for writers attempting to translate jargon into plain English.

Lanham, Richard A. *Revising Prose.* New York: Charles Scribner's Sons, 1979.

Provides a text for focusing on stylistic revisions; suitable for advanced writing classes.

Lees, Elaine O. "Evaluating Student Writing." *College Composition and Communication* 30 (December 1979): 370–74.

Explores the role of teacher as commentator and suggests seven modes of commentary: correcting, emoting, describing, suggesting, questioning, reminding, and assigning.

Little, Marjorie D., Susan C. Smith, and Margaret P. Wyszkowski. *Humanistic Response to Writing: One Means of Encouraging Growth in Student Writers through Evaluation.* Curriculum Publication No. 1. Las Cruces: New Mexico State Writing Institute, 1980.

Provides a number of sample student essays that have been annotated but not graded by teachers; comments suggest the various levels of response that teachers can use to help students view their writing as a part of an ongoing revision process.

Luban, Nina, Ann Matsuhashi, and Tom Reigstad. "One-to-One to Write: Establishing an Individual-Conference Writing Place." *English Journal* 67 (November 1978): 30–35.

Describes how to establish a center where students can go for individual conferences with teachers about writing; gives suggestions about ways of conducting a conference and about resources and facilities needed in the center.

Lynch, Catherine, and Patricia Klemans. "Evaluating Our Evaluations." *College English* 40 (October 1978): 166–70, 175–80.

Reports on a survey of student attitudes toward comments written on their papers and offers advice to teachers about the writing of comments.

Macrorie, Ken. "The Helping Circle." In *Telling Writing,* pp. 73–88. 3d ed. Rochelle Park, N.J.: Hayden Book Co., 1980.

Offers an anecdotal account of helping students become comfortable with the responses of small groups to their writing.

Maimon, Elaine P. "Talking to Strangers." *College Composition and Communication* 30 (December 1979): 364–69.

Suggests that the writing teacher often plays the role of sympathetic reader who helps the student work through multiple drafts in shaping a finished product ready for a stranger's eyes.

Mandel, Barrett J. "Losing One's Mind: Learning to Write and Edit." *College Composition and Communication* 29 (December 1978): 362–68.

Asserts that editing is seeing to it that what is written observes the conventions and rules agreed upon between writer and readers so that the written piece can be received and judged by the readers without the distractions of faulty punctuation, poor spelling, and other errors.

McDonald, W. U., Jr. "The Revising Process and the Marking of Student Papers." *College Composition and Communication* 29 (May 1978): 167–70.

Argues that commenting upon preliminary drafts of student papers as well as final versions is helpful. Comments on preliminary drafts should focus on fundamental problems, leaving others for later consideration.

McFarland, Betty. "Writing and Proofreading: An Alternative Program for Basic Composition Courses." Paper presented at the annual meeting of the Southeastern Conference on English in the Two-Year College, Nashville, Tennessee, February 1977. (ERIC Document Reproduction Service No. ED 150 618).

Describes a writing course based on a personalized system of instruction (PSI model) that calls for self-paced instruction; proofreading is integrated with writing and only major errors are emphasized.

Murray, Donald M. "Internal Revision: A Process of Discovery." In *Research on Composing: Points of Departure,* edited by Charles R. Cooper and Lee Odell, pp. 85–103. Urbana, Ill.: National Council of Teachers of English, 1978.

Identifies two kinds of revision: external revision (preparing the writing for a reader) and internal revision (discovering meaning, structure, preferred word choices, voice in what one has written).

Murray, Donald M. "The Listening Eye: Reflections on the Writing Conference." *College English* 41 (September 1979): 13–18.

Offers a personal account of how students eventually accept responsibility for the focus and development of a writing conference.

Murray, Donald M. "Teach the Motivating Force of Revision." *English Journal* 67 (October 1978): 56–60.

Provides a rationale for why revision may be one of the strongest motivators for getting students to write, with a distinction between internal and external revision.

Murray, Donald M. "Writing Process/Response Exercise." *Exercise Exchange,* Fall 1979, pp. 61–63.

Outlines an exercise that takes the writer through the entire writing process in approximately thirty-five minutes and shows how the exercise reinforces the various stages of the process by using peer response and revision techniques.

Newman, Barbara J. "Peer Evaluation in Teaching Composition." *Ohio English Language Arts Bulletin,* Winter/Spring 1980, pp. 61–64.

Recounts how the author discovered peer evaluation techniques and put them to use to increase student awareness of the need for revision within the writing process.

Nold, Ellen W. "Revising: Toward a Theory." Paper presented at the annual meeting of the Conference on College Composition and Communication, Minneapolis, Minnesota, April 1979. (ERIC Document Reproduction Service No. ED 172 212).

Places revision within a general theory of the writing process and shows how studies that ignore the entire process obscure rather than add to our understanding of revising.

Odell, Lee, and Joanne Cohick. "You Mean, Write It Over in Ink?" *English Journal* 64 (December 1975): 48–53.

Describes six weeks of work with ninth-graders in which students were first given practice in asking questions about their subjects and in varying the focus used in describing; then they were trained to employ in the revision of papers certain discovery procedures developed by Richard Young, Alton Becker, and Kenneth Pike.

O'Donnell, Cathy. "Peer Editing: A Way to Improve Writing." Paper presented at the combined annual meeting of the Secondary English Section Conference and the Conference on English Education, Omaha, Nebraska, March 1980. (ERIC Document Reproduction Service No. ED 189 604).

Analyzes the characteristics of peer editing and suggests techniques to be used with peer editing groups.

Palumbo, Roberta M. "Revise! More Than a Command." *Exercise Exchange,* Fall 1977, pp. 33–36.

Recommends a process by which students learn to revise their own papers by using a series of guidelines and questions.

Pechar, George M. "An Evaluation of an Oral Proofreading Technique Used to Teach Grammar and Composition." Ed. D. dissertation, University of Kansas, 1976.

Concludes that an oral proofreading technique did not cause the writing of students who used it to be more free of errors than the writing of students who did not use it.

Peckham, Levin. "Peer Evaluation." *English Journal* 67 (October 1978): 61–63.

Outlines classroom procedures for introducing and carrying on peer evaluation activities that lead to revision.

Pferrer, Suzanne. "The Effect of Multiple Revision on Freshman Writing." Paper presented at the annual meeting of the Conference on College Composition and Communication, Washington, D.C., March 1980. (ERIC Document Reproduction Service No. ED 191 048).

Suggests how to help students change writer-centered drafts to reader-based prose.

Primeau, Ronald. "Film-Editing and the Revision Process: Student as Self-Editor." *College Composition and Communication* 25 (December 1974): 405–10.

Proposes that students first record notes, perceptions, ideas, and ways of viewing a subject; then students should arrange, shape, and synthesize what they have recorded, discarding some information in the process of constructing a new whole.

Rogalski, William. "Magazine Advertisement Analysis: A Group Approach to Rewriting." *Exercise Exchange,* Fall 1979, pp. 24–26.

Outlines a four-stage writing experience that emphasizes that rewriting often involves radical shifts in focus, addition and deletion of information, and reordering of paragraphs.

Sager, Carol. "Sager Writing Scale." From "Improving the Quality of Written Composition through Pupil Use of Rating Scale." Ed. D. dissertation, Boston University, 1973. (ERIC Document Reproduction Service No. ED 091 723).

Although designed to assess the quality of creative writing in the intermediate and junior high grades, the scale has potential for use by students as a guide for revision.

Sager, Carol. "Improving the Quality of Written Composition through Pupil Use of Rating Scale." Paper presented at the annual convention of the National Council of Teachers of English, Philadelphia, Pennsylvania, November 1973. (ERIC Document Reproduction Service No. ED 089 304).

Describes a program in which students learned to use a descriptive writing scale so they could rate their own compositions and those of other students.

Sherwood, Phyllis. "Nonlinear Revising." Paper presented at Wyoming Conference on Teaching Freshman and Sophomore English, Laramie, July 1980.

Suggests that revision can be prompted by ongoing evaluation by the writer during the writing process and that such revision can be encouraged by classroom activities.

Shuman, R. Baird. "What about Revision?" *English Journal* 64 (December 1975): 41–43.

Briefly reviews ways of looking at revision and offers strategies for encouraging revision.

Smith, Myrna J., and Barbara A. Bretcko. "Research on Individual Composition Conferences." Paper presented at the annual meeting of the Conference on College Composition and Communication, Anaheim, California, April 1974. (ERIC Document Reproduction Service No. ED 091 709).

Reports on a study in which students were involved in six conferences on their writing; beyond the first two, students did not seem to learn any more than if they spent the time in class.

Snipes, Wilson Currin. "Oral Composing as an Approach to Writing." *College Composition and Communication* 24 (May 1973): 200–205.

Summarizes the kinds of experiences that most eighteen-year-olds have had in using language and then argues for beginning instruction in written composition by asking students to compose orally—an approach labeled by the author as "talking-retalking-writing-rewriting."

Sommers, Nancy. "Revision in the Composing Process: A Case Study of College Freshmen and Experienced Adult Writers." Ed. D. dissertation, Boston University, 1978.

Examines the revision process as a sequence of changes in a piece of writing and identifies the operations used by experienced and inexperienced writers during revision.

Sommers, Nancy. "Revision Strategies of Student Writers and Experienced Adult Writers." *College Composition and Communication* 31 (December 1980): 378-88; see also "Revision Strategies of Student Writers and Experienced Writers." *Ohio English Language Arts Bulletin,* Winter/Spring 1980, pp. 8-14.

Presents arguments for looking at revision as an ongoing part of the writing process rather than as an isolated step at the end of the process. Compares student perceptions about revision with those of experienced writers.

Stanford, Gene, ed. *How to Handle the Paper Load.* Classroom Practices in Teaching English 1979-1980. Urbana, Ill.: National Council of Teachers of English, 1979.

Offers in sections on student self-editing and alternative audiences practical ways to engage students in revision.

Stine, Peter W. "Listen, My Children, and You Shall Hear: An Oral Approach to Correcting Written Errors." Paper presented at the annual meeting of the Conference on College Composition and Communication, Kansas City, Missouri, March 1977. (ERIC Document Reproduction Service No. ED 144 106).

Argues that oral reading can be an effective method for sensitizing students to the presence of grammatical and logical errors; limitations of the approach as well as applications for small-group and one-to-one teaching situations are discussed.

Thompson, George J. "Revision: Nine Ways to Achieve a Disinterested Perspective." *College Composition and Communication* 29 (May 1978): 200-202.

Suggests how students can "distance" themselves from their drafts and view their writing more objectively for revision.

Tschumy, Ruth D. "A Return to the Draft: Or, How to Wage War on the Nonreviser." *Arizona English Bulletin* 22 (February 1980): 157-61.

Recommends a draft-assessment-draft sequence where emphasis is placed on work in progress and comments place the responsibility for revision on the writer, not the teacher.

Van Dusen, Gerald C. "Teaching the Process of Editing." D. A. dissertation, University of Michigan, 1977.

Discusses ways of helping students understand the editing process, the use of editorial groups, the use of a diagnostic model for classifying errors, and the self-management phase of editing.

Woodman, Leonora. "Creative Editing: An Approach to Peer Criticism." Paper presented at the annual convention of the National Council of Teachers of English, San Diego, California, November 1975. (ERIC Document Reproduction Service No. ED 116 217).

Describes a method for teaching the nonnarrative essay to determine if students can provide informed editorial guidance to other students in peer criticism sessions.

Write/Rewrite: An Assessment of Revision Skills: Selected Results from the Second National Assessment of Writing. Education Commission of the States, Denver, Colorado, National Assessment of Educational Progress, Report No. 05-W-04. Washington, D.C.: U.S. Government Printing Office, 1977. (ERIC Document Reproduction Service No. ED 141 826).

Reviews a nationwide assessment of how young writers revise, with analyses of revisions by nine-, thirteen-, and seventeen-year-olds.

Young, Richard, Alton L. Becker, and Kenneth L. Pike. "Editing: Plots in Discourse" and "Editing: Focus and Loading." In *Rhetoric: Discovery and Change,* pp. 317–58. New York: Harcourt Brace Jovanovich, 1970.

Identifies a heuristic procedure that may be used as a guide for editing; includes examples and exercises.

Contributors

Richard Beach is Associate Professor of English Education at the Twin Cities Campus of the University of Minnesota. In addition to articles on writing and response to literature, he is the author of *Writing about Ourselves and Others,* coauthor of *Literature and the Reader,* and coeditor of *Perspectives on Literacy.* Professor Beach has served the National Council of Teachers of English in several capacities, among them his contributions to the Committee on Research and the Conference on English Education.

C. A. Daiute is Adjunct Assistant Professor and Research Associate at Teachers College, Columbia University. Among the courses she teaches are Computers and Writing, the use of computer text editing systems, and Computers and the Language Arts, which presents software for teaching writing, grammar, and literature. In 1980 Professor Daiute received the Promising Researcher in English Education Award from the National Council of Teachers of English.

Ken Davis, Associate Professor of English at the University of Kentucky, has coauthored the writing texts in Scholastic's *Real World English* series and NCTE's *Inventing and Playing Games in the English Classroom.* His book *Writing That Gets Things Done: A Process Approach to Business Writing* will be published in 1983 by Charles E. Merrill. Professor Davis is editor of the *Kentucky English Bulletin* and serves on the Board of Consultant-Evaluators of the Council of Writing Program Administrators.

Robert J. Denn has taught English and scientific writing at Northeastern University and at Michigan State University. He is now a software technical writer with Digital Equipment Corporation in Merrimack, New Hampshire.

Charles R. Duke, Professor of English at Murray State University, serves as Director of Freshman English and teaches courses in writing, English methods, and adolescent literature. In addition to many articles on the teaching of writing and literature, he has written three books on the teaching of English: *Creative Dramatics and English Teaching, Teaching Fundamental English Today,* and *Teaching Literature Today.* Professor Duke is Director of the West Kentucky Writing Project and President of the Kentucky Council of Teachers of English. In addition, he is editor of *Exercise Exchange,* a professional journal for English teachers published at Murray State.

Toby Fulwiler has taught at the University of Wisconsin–Madison and is currently Assistant Head of the Department of Humanities at Michigan Technological University. With Arthur Young he is editor of *Language Connections: Writing and Reading across the Curriculum.* Author of several articles on interdisciplinary writing, Professor Fulwiler has also conducted writing workshops in Wisconsin, Michigan, and Pennsylvania and at NCTE conventions and conferences.

Anne Ruggles Gere, Associate Professor of English at the University of Washington, is Director of the Puget Sound Writing Program. Author of numerous articles in NCTE journals, she is a member of the Secondary Section Steering Committee and coauthor, with Eugene Smith, of *Attitudes, Language, and Change.*

Robert Gregory is Assistant Professor in the English Department at Carnegie-Mellon University. His "Reading as Narcissism; *Le Roman de la Rose*" is forthcoming in *Sub-Stance.*

Karen Hodges is Coordinator of Basic Skills at the University of Arkansas. She has conducted in-service teacher workshops in North Carolina and Oklahoma on teaching revision as part of the composing process and published, with Christopher Gould, "The Art of Revision: An Annotated Bibliography" in *Style,* no. 2, 1981.

Daniel Marder teaches at the University of Tulsa. He has been a correspondent for *Time* and *Life,* news editor for Carnegie-Mellon University, and a speech writer for Bell Telephone. Professor Marder has been a Fulbright Professor at the University of Skopje, Yugoslavia, a visiting scholar at Cambridge University, and a visiting professor at the University of Keele, England. A frequent contributor to journals of rhetoric, literature, and technical and professional writing, he is the author of *The Craft of Technical Writing* and *College English.*

Edmund Miller teaches English at the C. W. Post Center of Long Island University. He is the author of *Drudgerie Divine: The Rhetoric of God and Man in George Herbert* and of numerous articles in such journals as *Christianity and Literature, College Literature, Victorian Newsletter, Armchair Detective,* and *Missouri English Bulletin.*

Ellen W. Nold is Director of the Communications Project of the School of Engineering at Stanford University. She has studied writing and evaluation experimentally, work derived from her "The Process of Writing," funded by a 1978 grant from the Exxon Education Foundation. She has written a book for teachers, *Managing Writing,* and coauthored with Brent Davis a book for students, *Writing in the Professions,* to be published by Scott, Foresman in 1983.

John J. Ruszkiewicz is Assistant Professor of English and Director of Freshman English at the University of Texas at Austin. In addition to articles on writing, he has written *Well-Bound Words: A Rhetoric.*

R. Baird Shuman, Professor of English at the University of Illinois at Urbana-Champaign, is Director of Freshman Rhetoric and Director of English Education. He has taught at the University of Pennsylvania, Drexel University, San José State University, and Duke University and has been a visiting professor at numerous institutions, among them Bread Loaf School of English of Middlebury College and King Faisal University in Saudi Arabia. Professor Shuman has published widely; his most recent book, *Education in the 80s: English,* was released in 1981 by the National Education Association.

Gayle L. Smith is Assistant Professor of English at the Worthington Scranton Campus of Pennsylvania State University. She has published articles on Emerson, on developmental composition, and on student grading.

Karen I. Spear teaches composition, literature, and liberal education at the University of Utah, where she is presently Assistant Dean of Liberal Education. She has published in *The Journal of Aesthetic Education, College Composition and Communication,* and *The Writing Center Journal.*

Ronald A. Sudol is Assistant Professor in the Department of Rhetoric, Communications, and Journalism at Oakland University. He has published articles on Emily Dickinson and on Colonial American literature and in conjunction with a task force of the Speech Communication Association is conducting research on presidential communication.

Ruth Windhover is Associate Professor in the English Department at the University of Idaho. She has directed its Writing Lab and served as codirector of the North Idaho Writing Project.